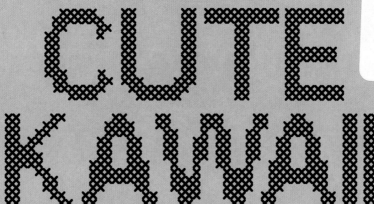

CUTE KAWAII

CROSS STITCH

OVER 400 SUPER-ADORABLE PATTERNS

Sosae & Dennis Caetano

DAVID & CHARLES

www.davidandcharles.com

A DAVID AND CHARLES BOOK
© Quarto Publishing plc 2023

David and Charles is an imprint of David and Charles, Ltd
Suite A, Tourism House, Pynes Hill, Exeter, EX2 5WS

Conceived, edited, and designed by Quarto Publishing, an imprint of
The Quarto Group, 1 Triptych Place, London, SE1 9SH

First published in the UK and USA in 2023

A catalogue record for this book is available from the British Library.

ISBN-13: 9781446309971 paperback
ISBN-13: 9781446309988 EPUB

This book has been printed on paper from approved suppliers and
made from pulp from sustainable sources.

Printed in China

10 9 8 7 6 5 4 3 2

Editor: Charlene Fernandes
Deputy art director: Martina Calvio
Designer: Karin Skånberg
Photography: Sosae and Dennis Caetano
Illustrator (page 9): Olya Kamieshkova
Managing editor: Lesley Henderson
Publisher: Lorraine Dickey

David and Charles publishes high-quality books on a wide range of
subjects. For more information visit www.davidandcharles.com.

Share your makes with us on social media using #dandcbooks and
follow us on Facebook and Instagram by searching for @dandcbooks.

Layout of the digital edition of this book may vary depending on
reader hardware and display settings.

Dedication

To Albert & Cynthia
and Hayastan & Seta

Thank you for all the love
and support.

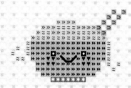

Contents

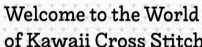

Welcome to the World of Kawaii Cross Stitch   10

Introduction

Welcome to the charming world of *Cute Kawaii Cross Stitch*! If you're like us, you're probably a fan of all things adorable. And perhaps you're an avid cross stitcher, or you're cross stitch-curious? Perfect. This book is for you. With over 400 motifs, from beginner to advanced skill levels, *Cute Kawaii Cross Stitch* is a veritable encyclopedia of kawaii cuteness.

When creating this book, we wanted to give you all kinds of fun designs to stitch. The nine chapters are divided into categories ranging from sweet critters to kitchen gadgets to seasonal favorites. If you can think of a kawaii cutie, it's probably in this book!

If you're new to cross stitch, our simple instructions will teach you everything you need to know to get started. So, jump right in and have fun—the wonderful world of *Cute Kawaii Cross Stitch* awaits!

Meet the Authors

Dennis and Sosae Caetano are a husband-and-wife design team, and fans of all things adorable. When they're not out gardening, they spend their days designing, writing, sewing, and stitching for their books and pattern company, Trellis & Thyme. Kawaii is their favorite cross-stitch style, and *Cute Kawaii Cross Stitch* celebrates their love of cuteness overload.

About This Book

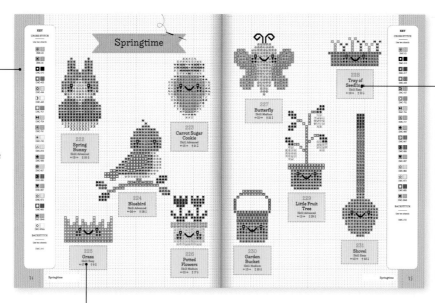

The color key shows you the symbols and colors used in each cross-stitch chart. DMC floss colors are provided for easy color matching.

Difficulty levels help you choose a pattern at your skill level. Easy patterns have larger single-color areas, whereas more advanced patterns require more color changes and have more intricate designs.

The dimensions for each design are given below each chart. Use this to choose the size of your aida fabric.

APPLICATIONS

Our favorite way of displaying kawaii cross stitch is to mount them in a small hoop and tie a ribbon (or twine) at the top for hanging. But here are some other neat ways to use and display your cross stitch cuties.

Ornaments: All the motifs in this book are sweet and small and suited perfectly for ornaments. Stitch a motif on a 4x4-inch square of aida. Then gently cut around the design, leaving one full square of space along the edge. Once it's cut out, trace it over a piece of colorful backing felt. Cut out the felt and glue it to the aida, inserting a ribbon for hanging up at the top.

Gift tags: Creating a gift tag with your cross stitch cutie is not much different from making an ornament. But instead of felt, use colorful craft paper, such as scrapbook paper, cut into a square or rectangle shape. Glue the cross stitch design to it. Punch a hole at the top to insert twine or ribbon.

Samplers: A cross stitch sampler is a large piece featuring different cross stitch motifs. You can have tons of fun here by choosing motifs from any of the themed chapters, and stitching them together onto one large (frameable!) piece of aida. You can even repeat the same motif. An In the Kitchen sampler would be great for—you guessed it—the kitchen! An Adorable Animals sampler would be darling for a child's bedroom. And seasonal samplers would be lovely to bring out each year with the changing holidays. Choose a workable number of motifs in an odd number; five would look lovely as a sampler displayed in a large hoop. Or, you can have your sampler framed at your local craft store.

Tools & Materials

One of the best things about cross stitch is how easy it is to get started. You only need a few tools, and they're readily available at craft stores and online.

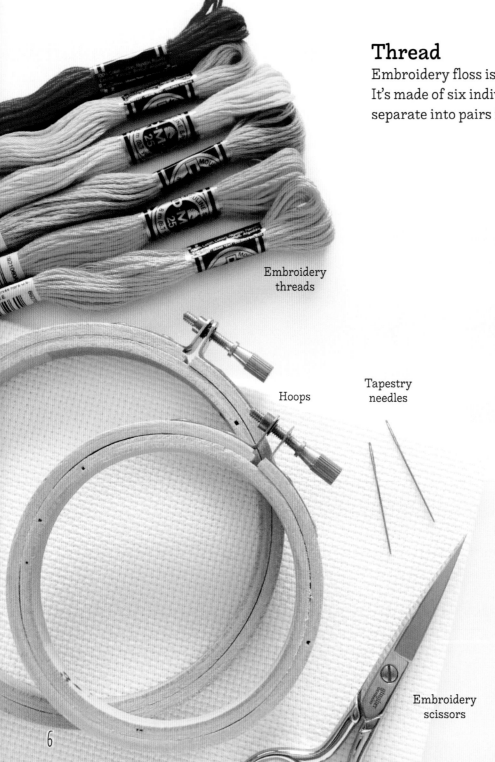

Embroidery threads

Hoops

Tapestry needles

Embroidery scissors

Thread
Embroidery floss is the best thread for cross stitch. It's made of six individual strands, which you will separate into pairs for stitching. (More on that later!)

Hoop
Hoops are wonderful for displaying finished pieces, and they can be helpful when stitching with lighter evenweave fabrics. When using aida, we prefer stitching without a hoop, as aida is sturdy and comfortable to hold directly in the hand.

Scissors
A sharp pair of scissors are a must for cross stitch. Choose embroidery scissors instead of large craft scissors, because they're smaller and able to cut fine thread with more precision.

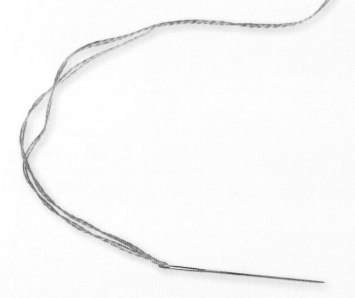

Needle

Unlike traditional embroidery, which uses a sharp-tipped needle, cross stitch requires a dull-tip tapestry needle. Why? Because aida already has holes in it, so you don't need a sharp needle to poke through the fabric. (In fact, a sharp needle may fray or tear your aida!) For 14-count aida, use a size 24 or 26 tapestry needle.

Fabric

Aida cloth is a sturdy, evenly woven fabric that looks like a grid. The size of the aida grid is determined by its count: 14, 16, and 18, for example. All the samples in this book are stitched on 14-count aida, which is the most popular. (It's also our favorite!) Aida comes in lots of pretty colors, and it's fun to pick the perfect color for your project. For example, if your motif has lots of white, choose a darker aida to make the stitches pop!

You can cross stitch on other kinds of fabric, too, such as evenweave cotton or linen. The grid counts can get very fine (28- and 32-count). We don't recommend this for beginner stitchers, as it takes a great deal of precision—and a good pair of reading glasses!

Aida

MOUNTING AIDA IN A HOOP IS EASY:

Loosen the metal screw to separate the inner and outer rings. Place your aida on top of the inner ring (you can hold it up to a light to see if your finished stitchwork is centered). Take the outer ring and align it over the aida and inner ring, and press down until it fits snugly, holding the aida between the two rings. Tighten the metal screw to hold your aida firmly in place. For displaying a single finished motif, a 3-inch hoop is perfect. If you're stitching more than one motif, use a 4-inch or larger hoop.

Before You Begin

If you're new to cross stitch, our simple instructions will teach you everything you need to know to get started.

Prep your fabric: Most motifs in this book fit a 4x4-inch aida square. For larger motifs, like the Tiger or Giraffe, cut a 6x6-inch piece of aida to give you more space around the motif. If your aida has any folds or creases, give it a gentle run with the iron on the "natural fiber" setting. Once it's crisp and flat, you're ready to go.

Prep your thread: Note which color you will start with, and cut an 18-inch length of embroidery floss. Embroidery floss has six strands, but you will only stitch with two at a time, so gently pull two strands away from the rest. Do this slowly so that nothing twists and tangles. (Put the remaining four strands aside to use later.) With your embroidery scissors, snip the ends of the thread to give you a crisp edge for fitting into the eye of the needle. Load the needle, and leave a 4-inch tail on one side. Don't knot your thread.

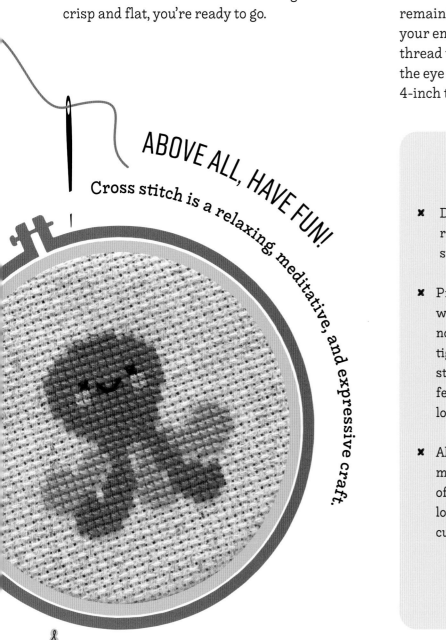

ABOVE ALL, HAVE FUN!
Cross stitch is a relaxing, meditative, and expressive craft.

CROSS STITCH TIPS

✖ Don't tug your stitches too tight, or you'll risk deforming the aida grid. You want the stitches to be snug and plump.

✖ Practice makes pretty. If your stitches look wonky and uneven, it means your tension is not consistent (some stitches are pulled too tight, others are left too loose.) To build even stitch tension, practice! After stitching a few kawaii cuties, you'll notice your stitches looking more uniform.

✖ Above all, have fun! Cross stitch is a relaxing, meditative, and expressive craft. The process of making those plump little "x" stitches is lots of fun, and so is watching your kawaii cutie come to life.

How to Cross Stitch

To cross stitch, you will follow a symbol-block chart, where each block corresponds to a DMC floss color and a position on the aida grid. Cross stitch is all about counting. (Don't worry, no algebra here.) It's easy and lots of fun.

Choose the motif you're going to stitch and locate its center. Now locate the center of your aida. You will count outward from the center and start at the lower right of the chart you're going to stitch. Count that same distance on your aida, and that's where you make your first stitch.

HOW TO MAKE "X" STITCHES

Cross stitches are made in two parts: First you will stitch a series of half cross stitches, and then you will come back and complete them.

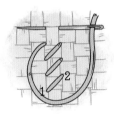

Bring your needle up from the back of the aida at Point 1 (leaving a 1-inch length of floss at the back for weaving in). Go back down at Point 2. Then come back up as shown in the illustration.

When you've reached the top of the column, bring your thread back up at Point 3 and back down at Point 4, completing one cross stitch. Continue this way until you complete all the cross stitches in the column.

HOW TO BACKSTITCH

Backstitch is the technique used to make the adorable kawaii smiles (and other details like steam.)

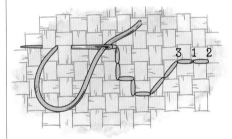

To backstitch, bring your needle up at Point 1 and then back down at Point 2. Bring it up again at Point 3 and then go back down at Point 1. Repeat.

Only use backstitch to add details once you have completed the cross stitch section of your motif.

HOW TO START A NEW THREAD

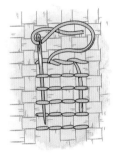

To start a new thread, weave it into a few stitches in the back, and you're ready to start stitching.

HOW TO CHANGE COLORS

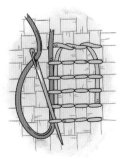

Changing floss colors is easy: Simply weave your working thread into a few stitches in the back and cut. (Don't knot your thread.)

WELCOME TO THE WORLD OF

Kawaii Cross Stitch

Fruit & Veggies

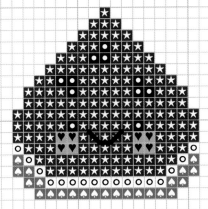

1
Watermelon
Skill: Medium
←17→ ↑17↓

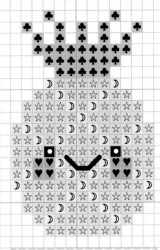

3
Pineapple
Skill: Advanced
←13→ ↑20↓

2
Fig
Skill: Medium
←16→ ↑16↓

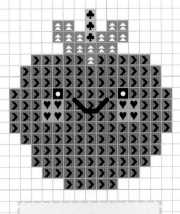

5
Raspberry
Skill: Easy
←15→ ↑16↓

4
Pear
Skill: Easy
←16→ ↑23↓

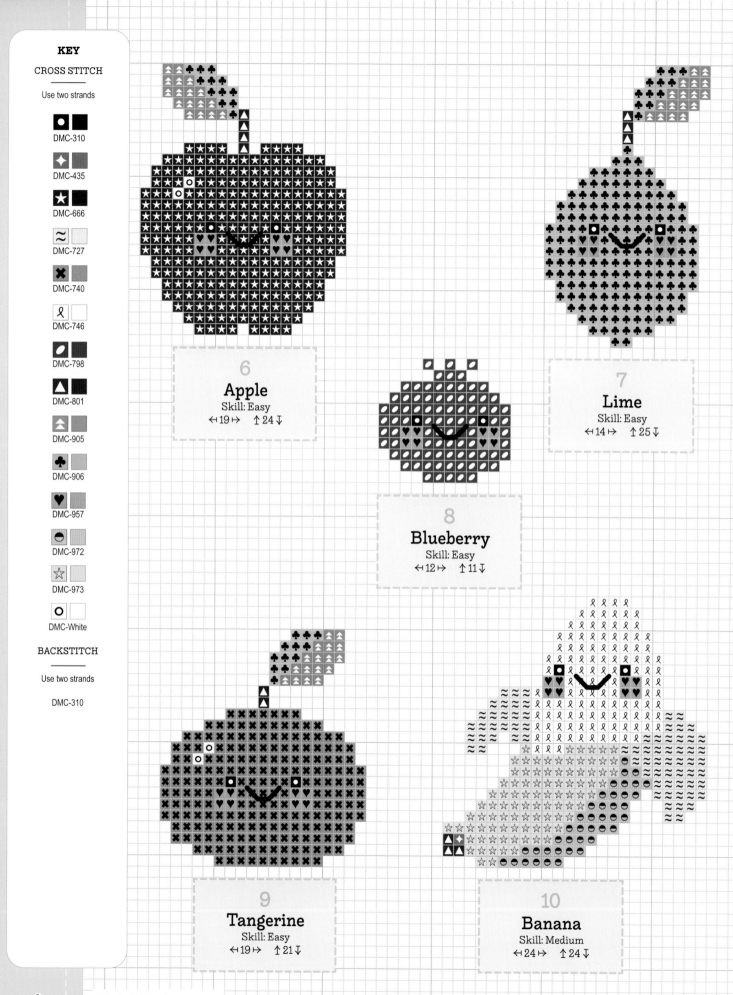

KEY

CROSS STITCH

Use two strands

DMC-310

DMC-435

DMC-666

DMC-727

DMC-740

DMC-746

DMC-798

DMC-801

DMC-905

DMC-906

DMC-957

DMC-972

DMC-973

DMC-White

BACKSTITCH

Use two strands

DMC-310

6
Apple
Skill: Easy
←19↦   ↑24↓

7
Lime
Skill: Easy
←14↦   ↑25↓

8
Blueberry
Skill: Easy
←12↦   ↑11↓

9
Tangerine
Skill: Easy
←19↦   ↑21↓

10
Banana
Skill: Medium
←24↦   ↑24↓

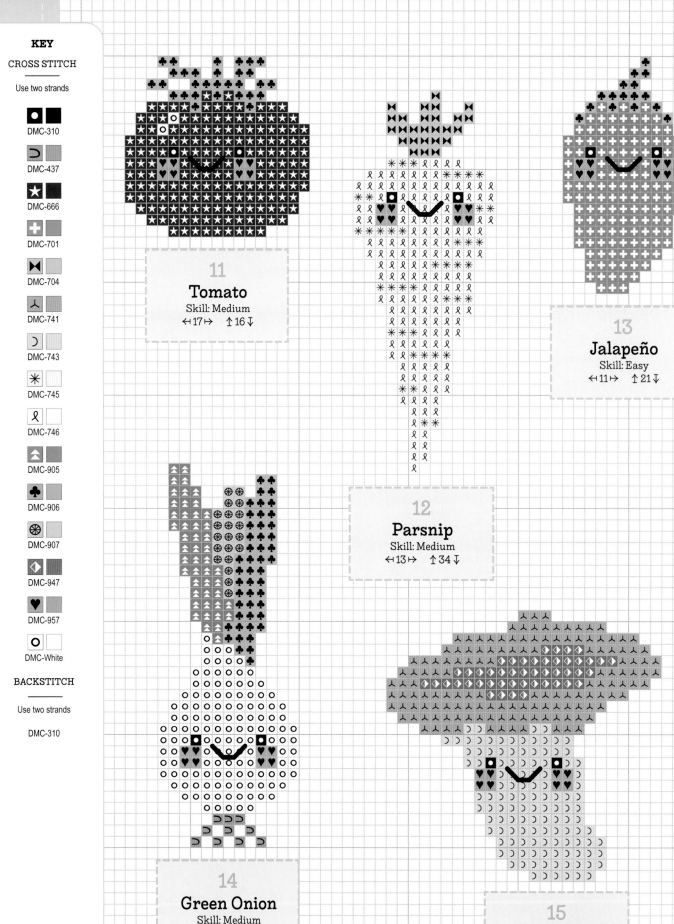

KEY

CROSS STITCH

Use two strands

▣ ■	DMC-310
⊃ ▧	DMC-437
★ ■	DMC-666
✚ ▨	DMC-701
⋈ ▨	DMC-704
⋏ ▨	DMC-741
⌒ ▨	DMC-743
✳ ▨	DMC-745
႙ ☐	DMC-746
⛰ ▨	DMC-905
♣ ▨	DMC-906
✺ ▨	DMC-907
◈ ▨	DMC-947
♥ ▨	DMC-957
◉ ☐	DMC-White

BACKSTITCH

Use two strands

DMC-310

11

Tomato
Skill: Medium
⟵17⟶ ⬆16⬇

13

Jalapeño
Skill: Easy
⟵11⟶ ⬆21⬇

12

Parsnip
Skill: Medium
⟵13⟶ ⬆34⬇

14

Green Onion
Skill: Medium
⟵13⟶ ⬆34⬇

15

Chanterelle
Mushroom
Skill: Medium
⟵25⟶ ⬆24⬇

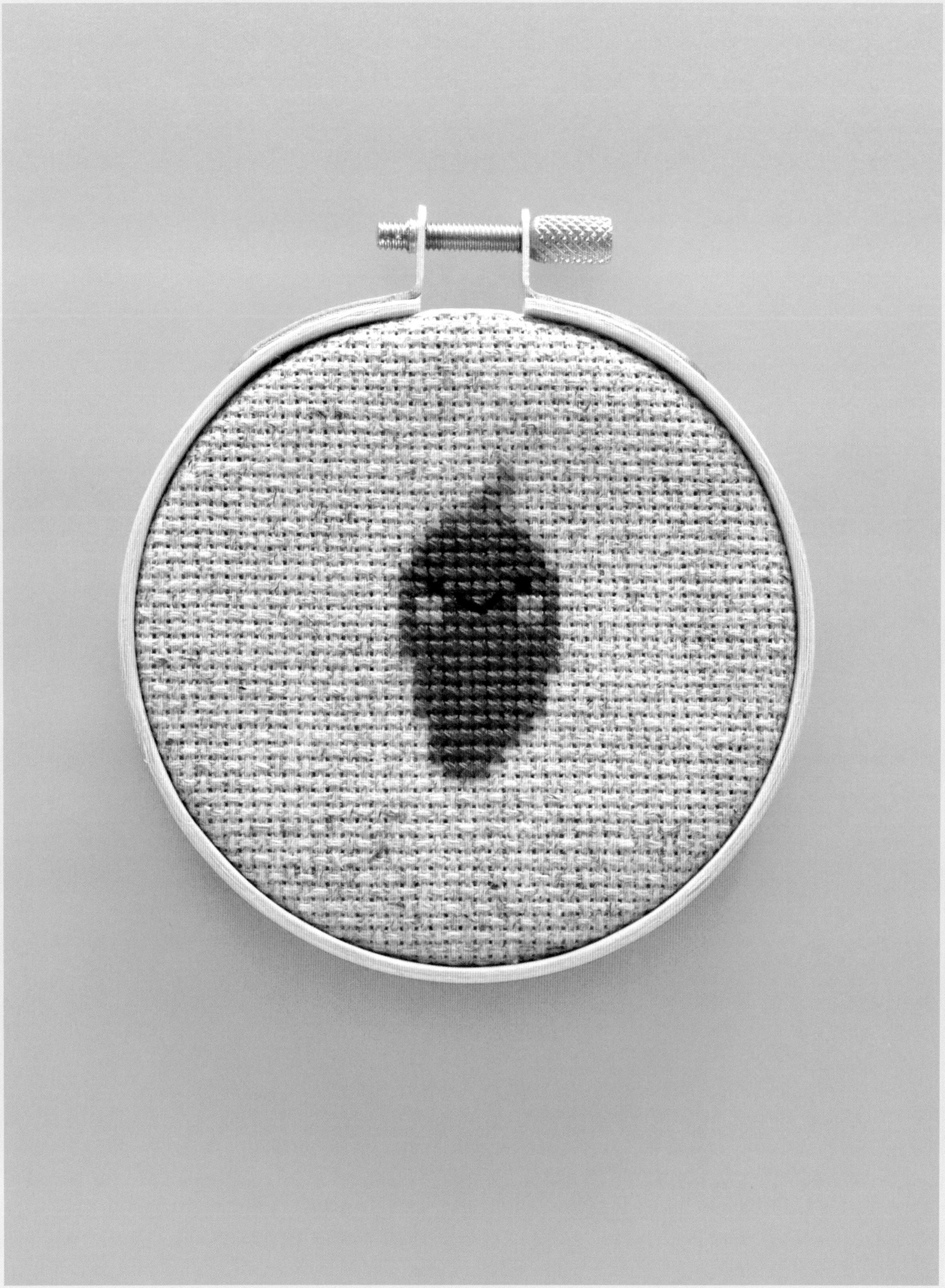

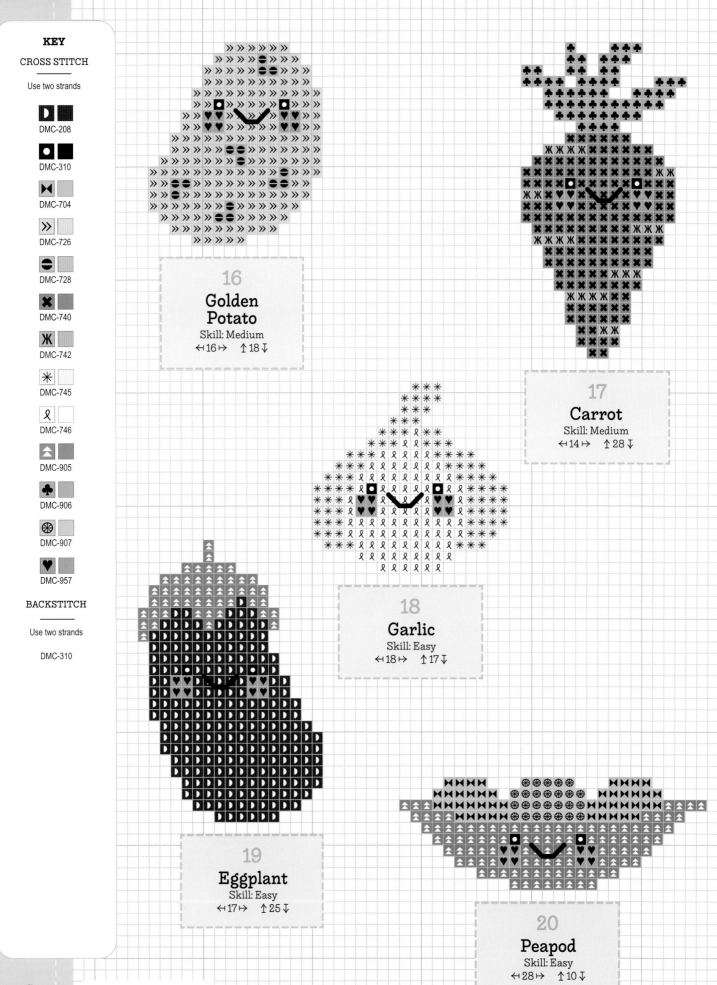

KEY

CROSS STITCH

Use two strands

DMC-208

DMC-310

DMC-704

DMC-726

DMC-728

DMC-740

DMC-742

DMC-745

DMC-746

DMC-905

DMC-906

DMC-907

DMC-957

BACKSTITCH

Use two strands

DMC-310

16
Golden Potato
Skill: Medium
←16↦ ↑18↓

17
Carrot
Skill: Medium
←14↦ ↑28↓

18
Garlic
Skill: Easy
←18↦ ↑17↓

19
Eggplant
Skill: Easy
←17↦ ↑25↓

20
Peapod
Skill: Easy
←28↦ ↑10↓

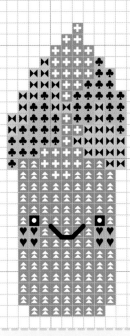

21

Asparagus

Skill: Advanced

←11↦ ↑26↓

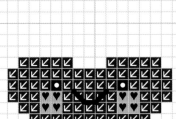

23

Cauliflower

Skill: Medium

←17↦ ↑14↓

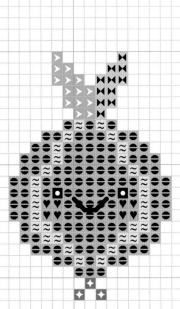

22

Kidney Bean

Skill: Easy

←15↦ ↑7↓

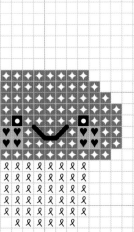

26

Turnip

Skill: Medium

←15↦ ↑18↓

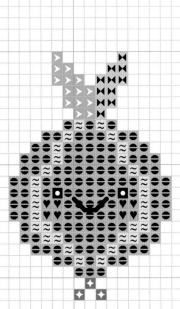

24

Onion

Skill: Advanced

←15↦ ↑22↓

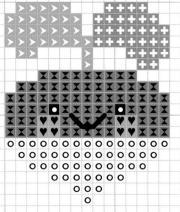

25

Button Mushroom

Skill: Easy

←14↦ ↑14↓

27
Artichoke
Skill: Advanced
←13→ ↑15↓

28
Avocado
Skill: Advanced
←17→ ↑19↓

29
Leek
Skill: Medium
←15→ ↑24↓

30
Bell Pepper
Skill: Easy
←17→ ↑19↓

31
Beet
Skill: Easy
←13→ ↑21↓

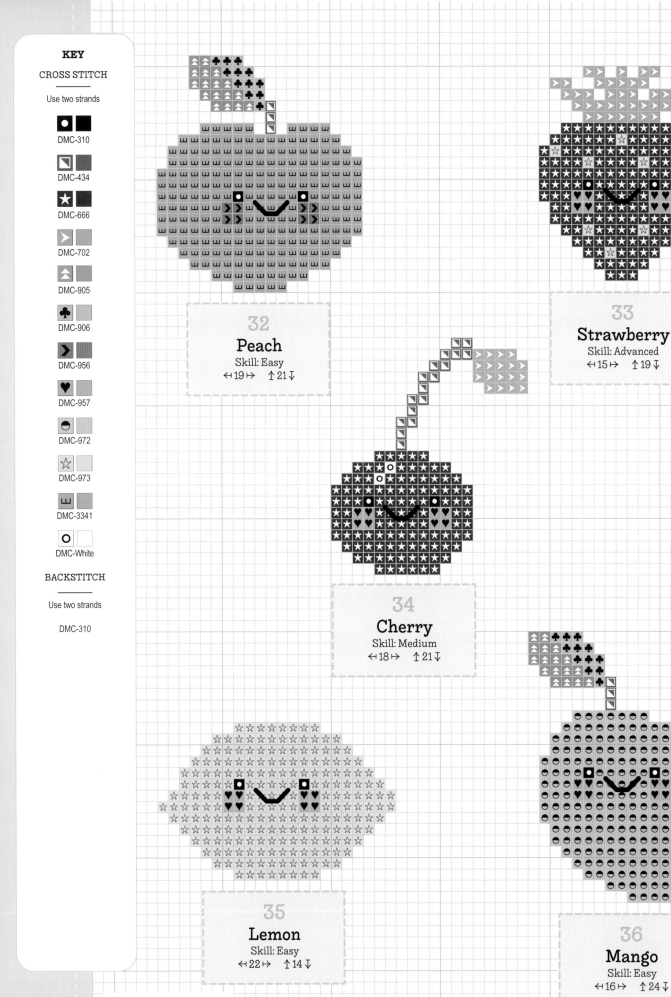

KEY

CROSS STITCH

Use two strands

DMC-310

DMC-434

DMC-666

DMC-702

DMC-905

DMC-906

DMC-956

DMC-957

DMC-972

DMC-973

DMC-3341

DMC-White

BACKSTITCH

Use two strands

DMC-310

32

Peach

Skill: Easy

←19→   ↑21↓

33

Strawberry

Skill: Advanced

←15→   ↑19↓

34

Cherry

Skill: Medium

←18→   ↑21↓

35

Lemon

Skill: Easy

←22→   ↑14↓

36

Mango

Skill: Easy

←16→   ↑24↓

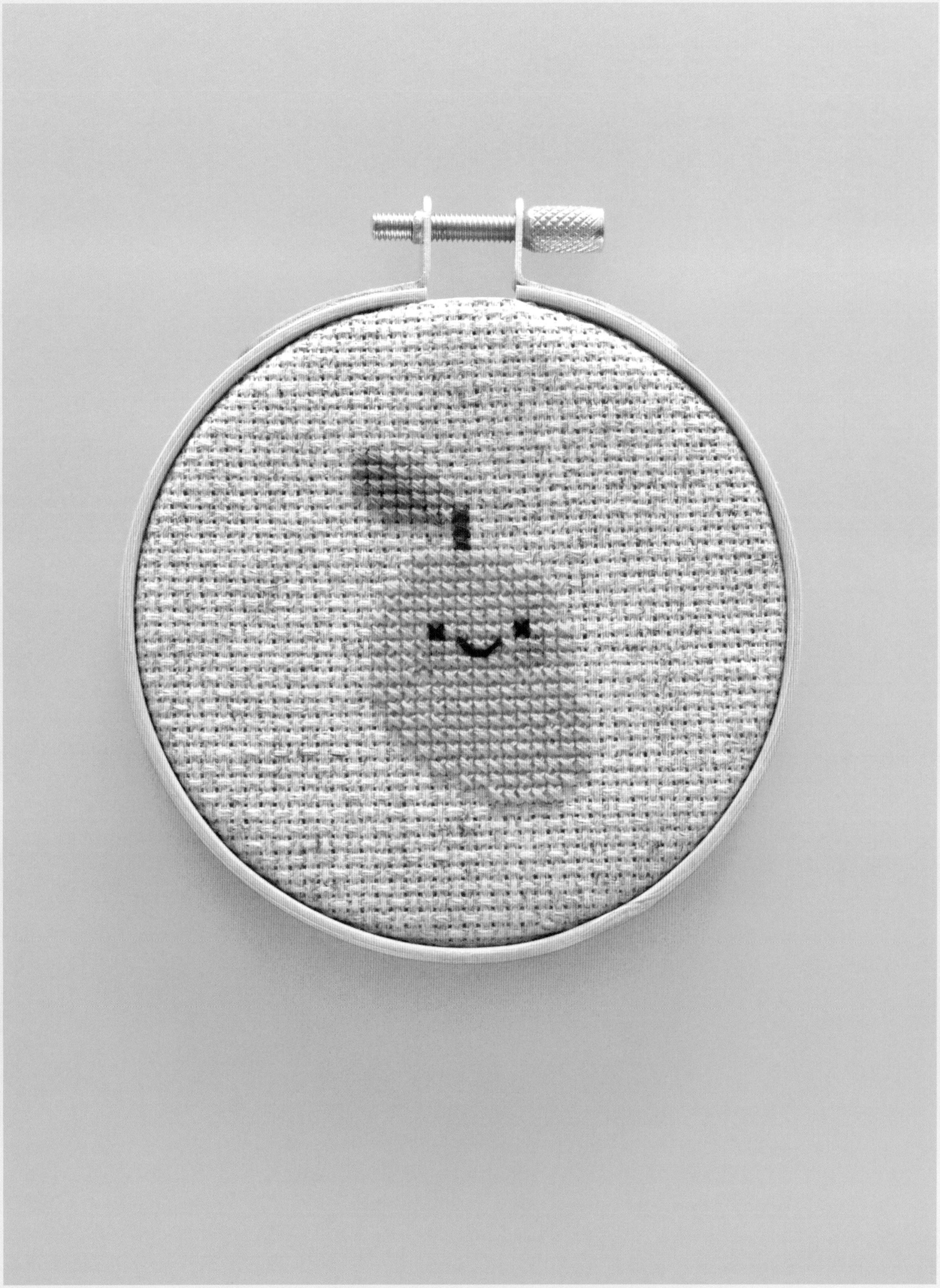

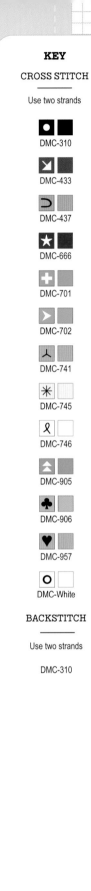

KEY

CROSS STITCH

Use two strands

- DMC-310
- DMC-433
- DMC-437
- DMC-666
- DMC-701
- DMC-702
- DMC-741
- DMC-745
- DMC-746
- DMC-905
- DMC-906
- DMC-957
- DMC-White

BACKSTITCH

Use two strands

DMC-310

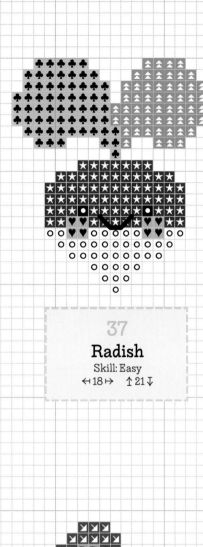

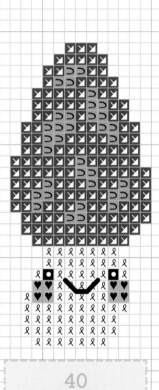

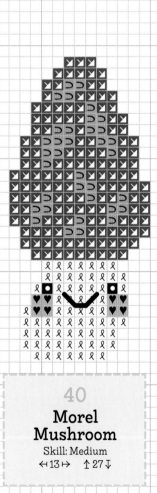

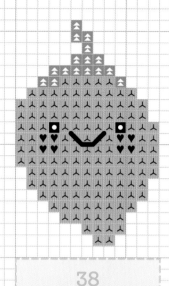

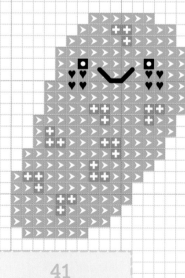

37
Radish
Skill: Easy
←18↦   ↑21↓

38
Habanero Pepper
Skill: Easy
←13↦   ↑20↓

39
Butternut Squash
Skill: Easy
←13↦   ↑19↓

40
Morel Mushroom
Skill: Medium
←13↦   ↑27↓

41
Cucumber
Skill: Medium
←16↦   ↑20↓

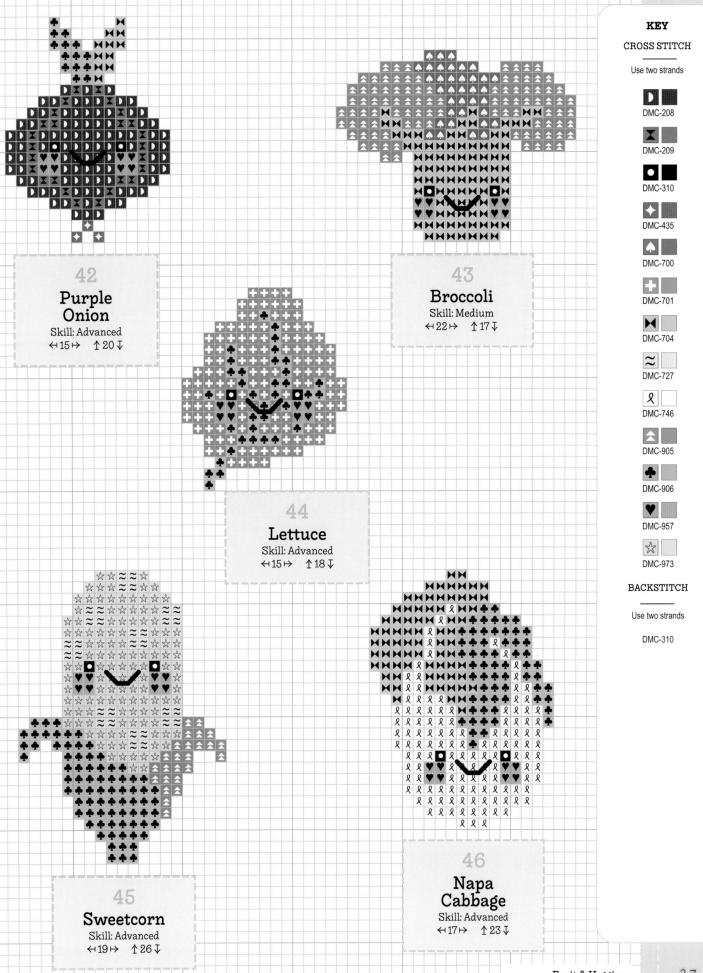

KEY

CROSS STITCH

Use two strands

DMC-208

DMC-209

DMC-310

DMC-435

DMC-700

DMC-701

DMC-704

DMC-727

DMC-746

DMC-905

DMC-906

DMC-957

DMC-973

BACKSTITCH

Use two strands

DMC-310

42

Purple Onion

Skill: Advanced

←15↦   ↑20↓

43

Broccoli

Skill: Medium

←22↦   ↑17↓

44

Lettuce

Skill: Advanced

←15↦   ↑18↓

45

Sweetcorn

Skill: Advanced

←19↦   ↑26↓

46

Napa Cabbage

Skill: Advanced

←17↦   ↑23↓

KEY

CROSS STITCH

Use two strands

DMC-03

DMC-310

DMC-434

DMC-435

DMC-437

DMC-666

DMC-702

DMC-726

DMC-727

DMC-746

DMC-782

DMC-801

DMC-828

DMC-957

DMC-973

DMC-White

BACKSTITCH

Use two strands

DMC-310

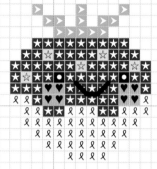

47
White Chocolate Strawberry
Skill: Advanced
←13↦ ↑14↓

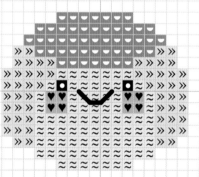

49
Flan
Skill: Easy
←17↦ ↑14↓

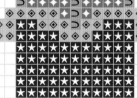

50
Chocolate Bar
Skill: Medium
←15↦ ↑17↓

48
Chocolate Chip Cookie
Skill: Medium
←16↦ ↑14↓

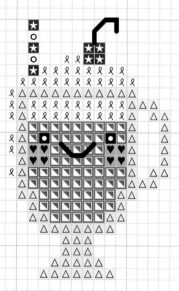

51
Rootbeer Float
Skill: Advanced
←15↦ ↑23↓

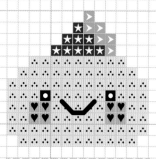

52
Strawberry Mochi
Skill: Easy
←13↦ ↑12↓

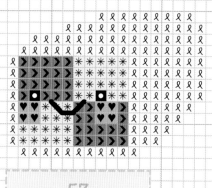

53
Battenberg Cake
Skill: Medium
←18↦ ↑13↓

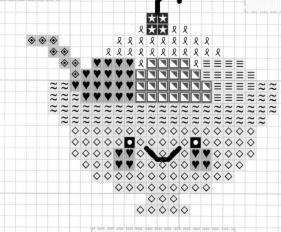

54
Banana Split
Skill: Advanced
←23↦ ↑20↓

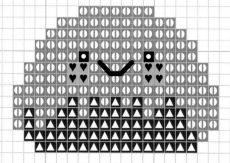

55
Sticky Toffee Pudding
Skill: Easy
←19↦ ↑13↓

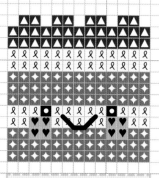

56
Tiramisu
Skill: Easy
←13↦ ↑13↓

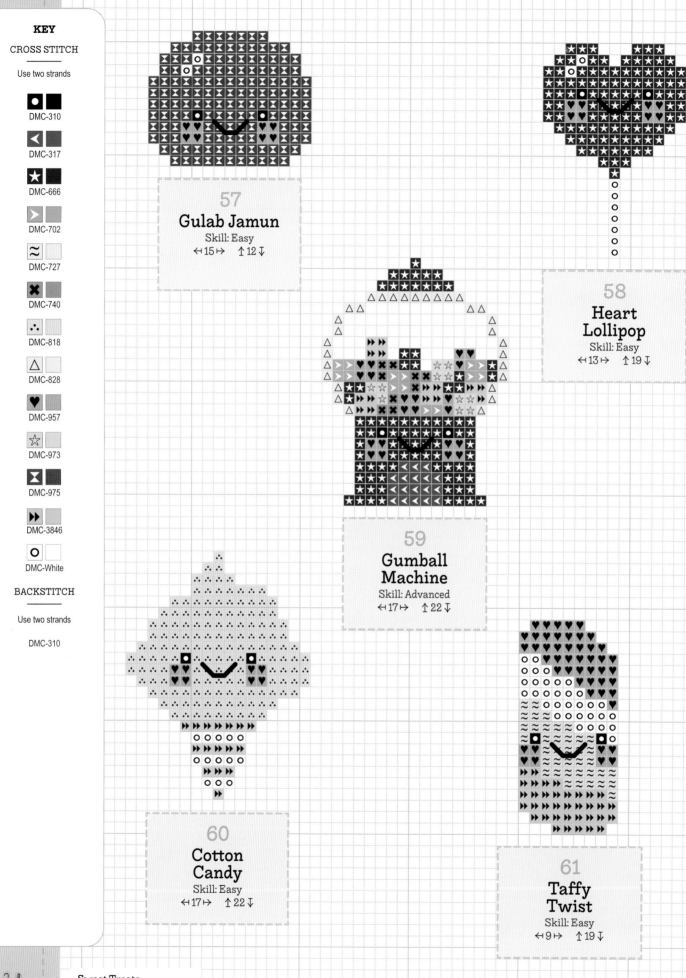

KEY

CROSS STITCH

Use two strands

DMC-310

DMC-317

DMC-666

DMC-702

DMC-727

DMC-740

DMC-818

DMC-828

DMC-957

DMC-973

DMC-975

DMC-3846

DMC-White

BACKSTITCH

Use two strands

DMC-310

57
Gulab Jamun
Skill: Easy
←15↦   ↑12↓

58
Heart Lollipop
Skill: Easy
←13↦   ↑19↓

59
Gumball Machine
Skill: Advanced
←17↦   ↑22↓

60
Cotton Candy
Skill: Easy
←17↦   ↑22↓

61
Taffy Twist
Skill: Easy
←9↦   ↑19↓

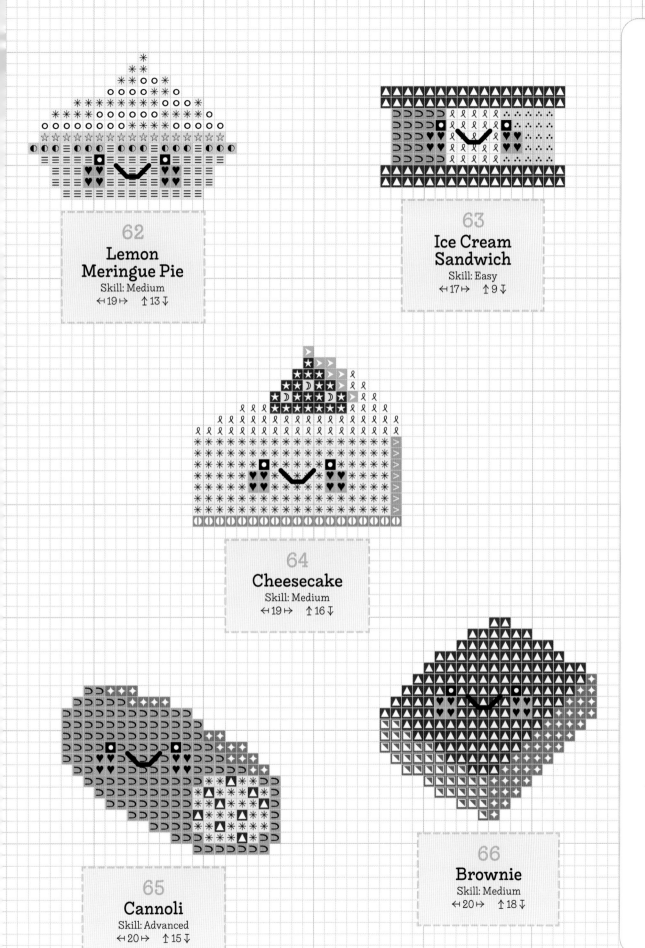

62

Lemon
Meringue Pie
Skill: Medium
←19→ ↑13↓

63

Ice Cream
Sandwich
Skill: Easy
←17→ ↑9↓

64

Cheesecake
Skill: Medium
←19→ ↑16↓

65

Cannoli
Skill: Advanced
←20→ ↑15↓

66

Brownie
Skill: Medium
←20→ ↑18↓

KEY

CROSS STITCH

Use two strands

DMC-310

DMC-434

DMC-435

DMC-437

DMC-445

DMC-666

DMC-676

DMC-702

DMC-745

DMC-746

DMC-781

DMC-783

DMC-801

DMC-818

DMC-955

DMC-957

DMC-973

DMC-White

BACKSTITCH

Use two strands

DMC-310

KEY

CROSS STITCH

Use two strands

 DMC-310

 DMC-437

 DMC-581

 DMC-666

 DMC-702

 DMC-738

 DMC-745

 DMC-746

 DMC-783

 DMC-801

 DMC-828

 DMC-954

 DMC-957

BACKSTITCH

Use two strands

DMC-310

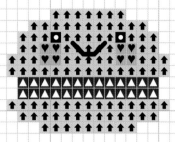

67
Macaron
Skill: Easy
←15↦ ↑11↓

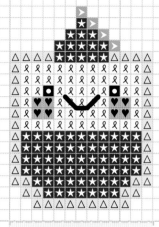

68
Jelly Custard
Skill: Advanced
←13↦ ↑18↓

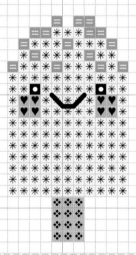

69
Kulfi
Skill: Medium
←11↦ ↑20↓

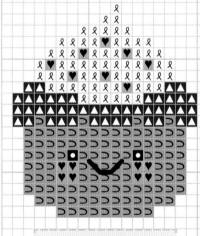

70
Frosted Cupcake
Skill: Medium
←17↦ ↑19↓

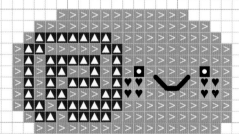

71
Kleicha
Skill: Advanced
←20↦ ↑11↓

KEY

CROSS STITCH

Use two strands

 DMC-310

 DMC-435

 DMC-437

 DMC-444

 DMC-666

 DMC-704

 DMC-727

 DMC-738

 DMC-741

 DMC-745

 DMC-956

 DMC-957

 DMC-973

 DMC-3846

 DMC-White

BACKSTITCH

Use two strands

DMC-310

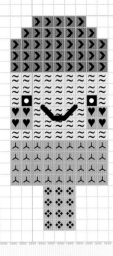

72
Popsicle
Skill: Easy
←9↦ ↑19↓

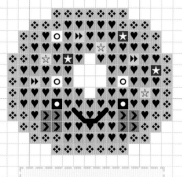

73
Donut
Skill: Advanced
←15↦ ↑13↓

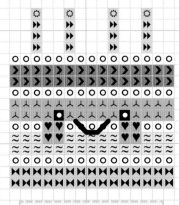

74
Birthday Cake
Skill: Medium
←15↦ ↑16↓

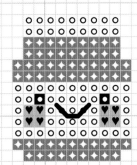

75
Hazelnut Spread
Skill: Easy
←11↦ ↑13↓

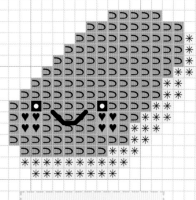

76
Maple Bar
Skill: Easy
←17↦ ↑15↓

Sweet Treats

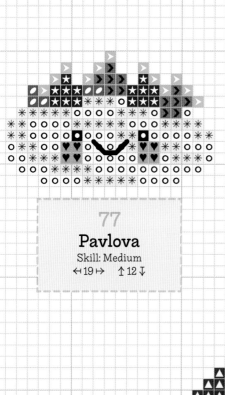

77
Pavlova
Skill: Medium
←19→ ↑12↓

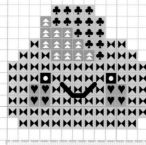

78
Green Tea Mochi
Skill: Easy
←13→ ↑11↓

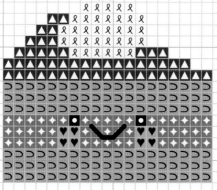

79
Cake Slice
Skill: Medium
←19→ ↑18↓

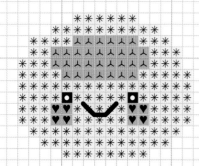

80
Jam Cookie
Skill: Easy
←16→ ↑13↓

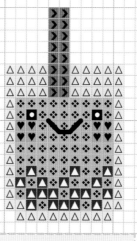

81
Boba Tea
Skill: Advanced
←11→ ↑19↓

82
Heart Sugar Cookie
Skill: Medium
←19↦   ↑17↓

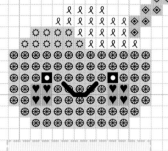

83
Mango Sticky Rice
Skill: Medium
←15↦   ↑12↓

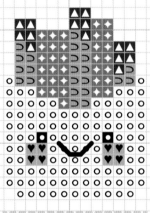

84
Churros
Skill: Medium
←13↦   ↑17↓

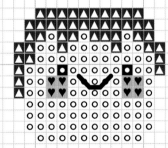

85
Chocolate Marshmallow
Skill: Easy
←14↦   ↑12↓

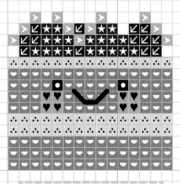

86
Strawberry Sponge
Skill: Advanced
←15↦   ↑14↓

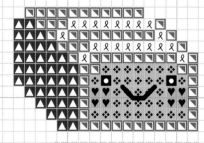

87
Chocolate Confection
Skill: Medium
←17↦ ↑11↓

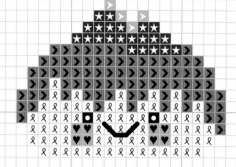

88
Panna Cotta
Skill: Medium
←19↦ ↑14↓

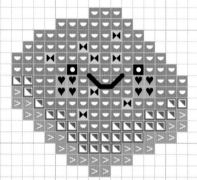

89
Baklava
Skill: Advanced
←16↦ ↑15↓

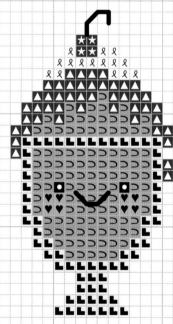

90
Fudge Sundae
Skill: Advanced
←15↦ ↑27↓

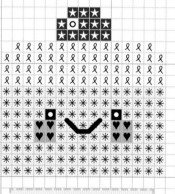

91
Tres Leches Cake
Skill: Easy
←15↦ ↑15↓

Yummy Food

92
Blueberry Muffin
Skill: Easy
←17→ ↑15↓

93
Jar of Honey
Skill: Medium
←17→ ↑15↓

94
Milk
Skill: Medium
←11→ ↑20↓

95
Maple Syrup
Skill: Medium
←13→ ↑20↓

96
Pancakes
Skill: Medium
←18→ ↑15↓

KEY

CROSS STITCH

Use two strands

 DMC-310

 DMC-434

 DMC-437

 DMC-666

 DMC-676

 DMC-726

 DMC-727

 DMC-741

 DMC-745

 DMC-780

 DMC-782

 DMC-783

 DMC-798

 DMC-828

 DMC-957

 DMC-White

BACKSTITCH

Use two strands

DMC-310

DMC-03

DMC-310

DMC-666

 DMC-727

DMC-738

DMC-740

DMC-741

DMC-742

DMC-745

DMC-780

DMC-781

DMC-783

DMC-798

DMC-828

DMC-956

DMC-957

DMC-995

DMC-3846

DMC-White

BACKSTITCH

Use two strands

DMC-310

98
Toaster Pastry
Skill: Easy
←11→ ↑13↓

97
Soft Boiled Egg
Skill: Easy
←13→ ↑20↓

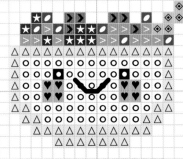

99
Fruit & Yogurt Bowl
Skill: Medium
←18→ ↑14↓

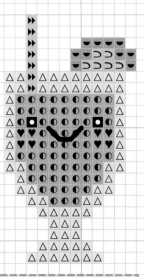

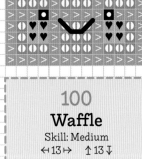

100
Waffle
Skill: Medium
←13→ ↑13↓

101
Orange Juice
Skill: Medium
←12→ ↑22↓

KEY

CROSS STITCH

Use two strands

○ ■ DMC-310

◩ DMC-434

✦ DMC-435

☼ DMC-444

★ DMC-666

▷ DMC-702

≫ DMC-726

≈ DMC-727

❖ DMC-738

✳ DMC-745

ℓ DMC-746

▷ DMC-783

▲ DMC-801

△ DMC-828

⬭ DMC-946

♥ DMC-957

BACKSTITCH

Use two strands

DMC-310

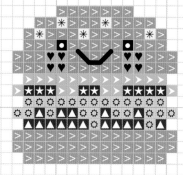

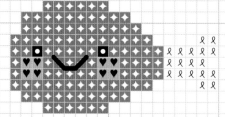

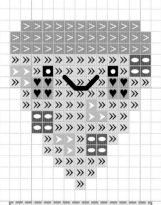

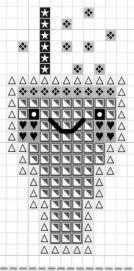

102
French Fries
Skill: Easy
←11↦   ↑14↓

103
Hamburger
Skill: Advanced
←15↦   ↑14↓

104
Chicken Leg
Skill: Easy
←19↦   ↑10↓

105
Pizza
Skill: Medium
←13↦   ↑15↓

106
Cola
Skill: Medium
←11↦   ↑22↓

CROSS STITCH

Use two strands

 DMC-04

 DMC-168

 DMC-310

 DMC-437

 DMC-444

 DMC-666

 DMC-702

 DMC-745

 DMC-746

 DMC-783

 DMC-801

 DMC-828

 DMC-957

 DMC-975

 DMC-White

BACKSTITCH

Use two strands

DMC-310

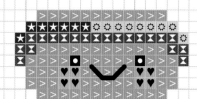

107
Hotdog
Skill: Medium
←16→ ↑8↓

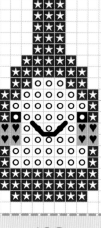

108
Ketchup
Skill: Medium
←9→ ↑20↓

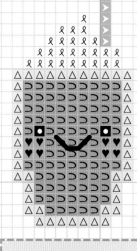

109
Iced Coffee
Skill: Medium
←11→ ↑21↓

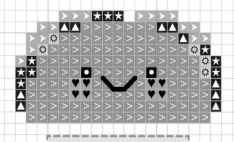

110
Taco
Skill: Medium
←19→ ↑10↓

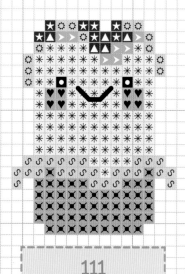

111
Burrito
Skill: Advanced
←15→ ↑19↓

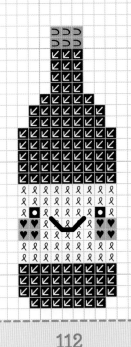

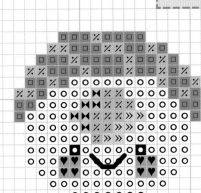

112
Red Wine
Skill: Easy
←9→   ↑25↓

113
Grilled Cheese Sandwich
Skill: Medium
←21→   ↑11↓

114
Sushi Roll
Skill: Advanced
←17→   ↑15↓

115
Milkshake
Skill: Advanced
←11→   ↑25↓

116
Avocado Toast
Skill: Easy
←13→   ↑15↓

KEY

CROSS STITCH

Use two strands

 DMC-310

 DMC-434

 DMC-437

 DMC-444

 DMC-666

 DMC-704

 DMC-726

 DMC-746

 DMC-782

 DMC-816

 DMC-828

 DMC-956

 DMC-957

DMC-3340

DMC-3824

DMC-3846

 DMC-White

BACKSTITCH

Use two strands

DMC-310

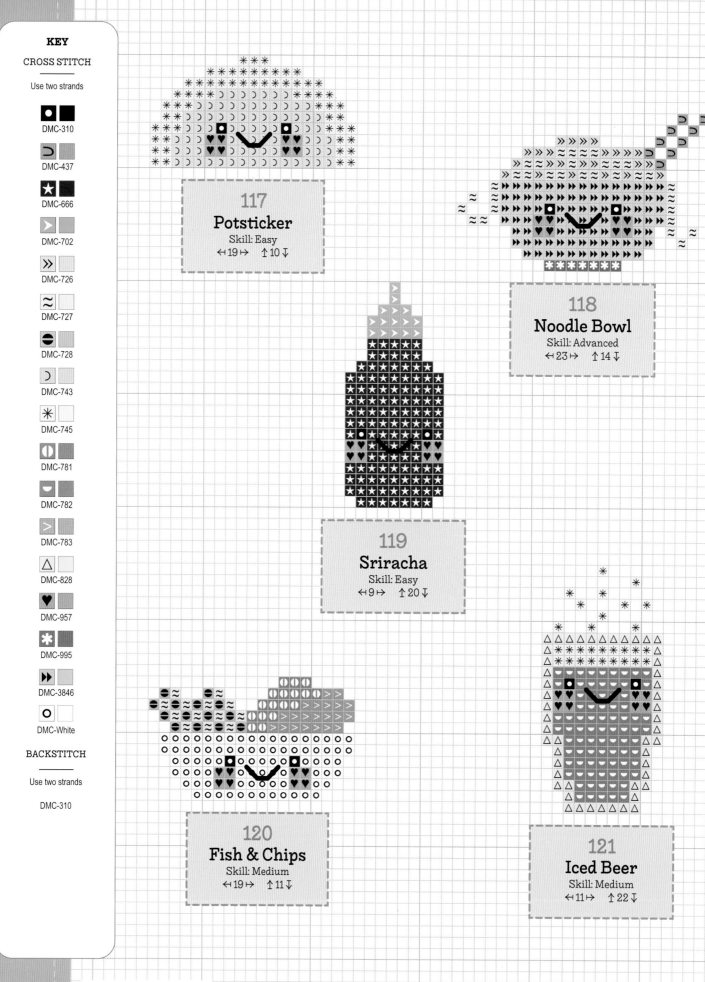

KEY

CROSS STITCH

Use two strands

DMC-310

DMC-437

DMC-666

DMC-702

DMC-726

DMC-727

DMC-728

DMC-743

DMC-745

DMC-781

DMC-782

DMC-783

DMC-828

DMC-957

DMC-995

DMC-3846

DMC-White

BACKSTITCH

Use two strands

DMC-310

117
Potsticker
Skill: Easy
← 19 →   ↑ 10 ↓

118
Noodle Bowl
Skill: Advanced
← 23 →   ↑ 14 ↓

119
Sriracha
Skill: Easy
← 9 →   ↑ 20 ↓

120
Fish & Chips
Skill: Medium
← 19 →   ↑ 11 ↓

121
Iced Beer
Skill: Medium
← 11 →   ↑ 22 ↓

122
Salad
Skill: Advanced
←18→ ↑15↓

123
Cheese
Skill: Medium
←15→ ↑12↓

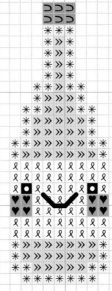

124
White Wine
Skill: Medium
←9→ ↑25↓

125
Dijon Mustard
Skill: Medium
←11→ ↑15↓

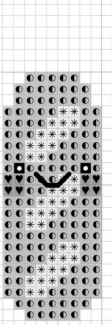

126
Baguette
Skill: Medium
←9→ ↑22↓

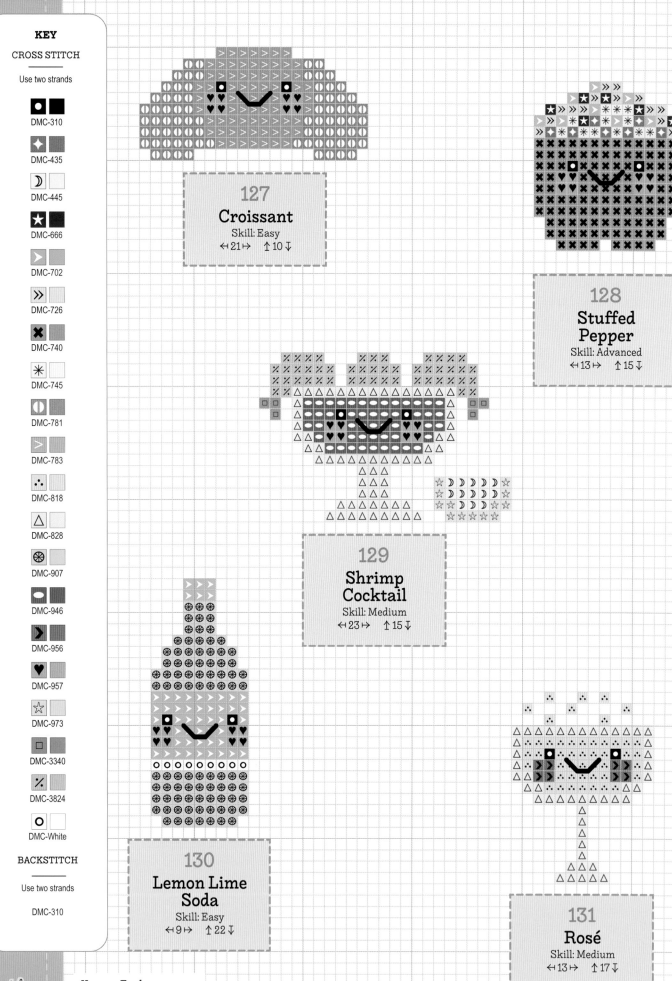

KEY

CROSS STITCH

Use two strands

■□ DMC-310

✦ DMC-435

☽ DMC-445

★ DMC-666

▶ DMC-702

» DMC-726

✖ DMC-740

✳ DMC-745

◖ DMC-781

> DMC-783

⁙ DMC-818

△ DMC-828

⊛ DMC-907

⬭ DMC-946

◗ DMC-956

♥ DMC-957

☆ DMC-973

▫ DMC-3340

⁒ DMC-3824

○ DMC-White

BACKSTITCH

Use two strands

DMC-310

127
Croissant
Skill: Easy
←21→   ↑10↓

128
Stuffed Pepper
Skill: Advanced
←13→   ↑15↓

129
Shrimp Cocktail
Skill: Medium
←23→   ↑15↓

130
Lemon Lime Soda
Skill: Easy
←9→   ↑22↓

131
Rosé
Skill: Medium
←13→   ↑17↓

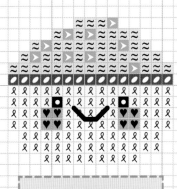

132
Mashed Potatoes
Skill: Medium
←15↦ ↑13↓

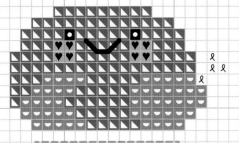

133
Kimchi
Skill: Advanced
←11↦ ↑16↓

134
Sub Sandwich
Skill: Medium
←23↦ ↑10↓

135
Roast Turkey
Skill: Medium
←20↦ ↑11↓

136
Flute of Champagne
Skill: Medium
←9↦ ↑27↓

KEY

CROSS STITCH
Use two strands

 DMC-04

 DMC-310

 DMC-435

 DMC-437

 DMC-666

 DMC-702

 DMC-704

 DMC-727

 DMC-741

 DMC-745

 DMC-746

 DMC-780

 DMC-782

 DMC-798

 DMC-828

 DMC-947

 DMC-957

 DMC-3855

BACKSTITCH
Use two strands

DMC-310

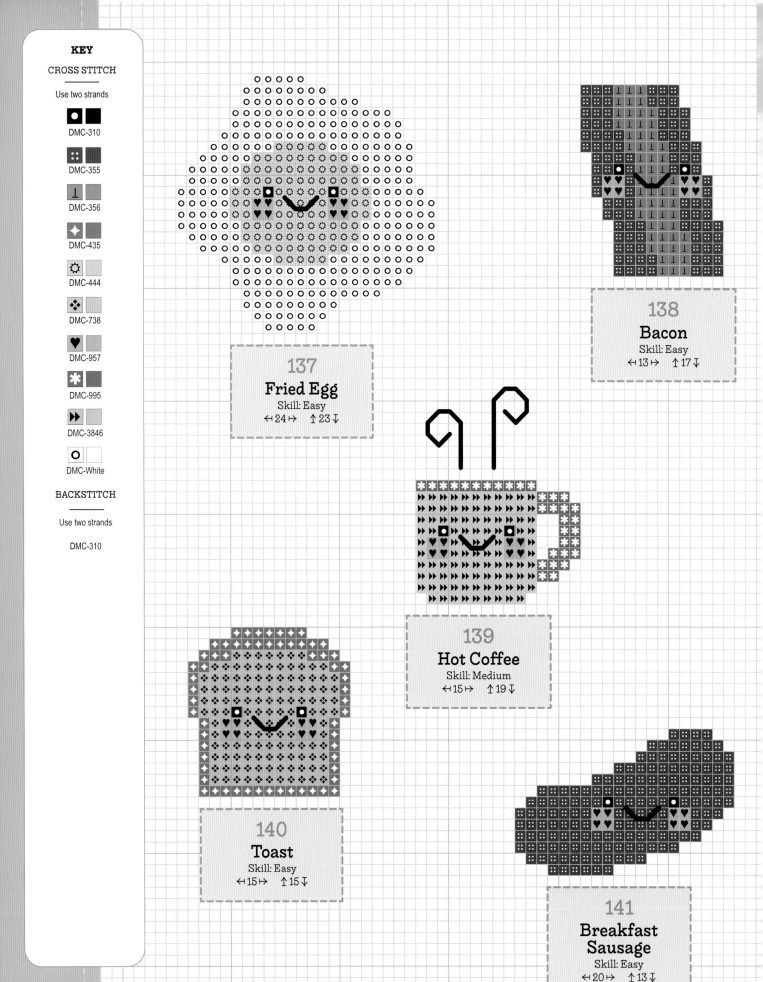

KEY

CROSS STITCH

Use two strands

DMC-310

DMC-355

DMC-356

DMC-435

DMC-444

DMC-738

DMC-957

DMC-995

DMC-3846

DMC-White

BACKSTITCH

Use two strands

DMC-310

137
Fried Egg
Skill: Easy
←24↦ ↑23↓

138
Bacon
Skill: Easy
←13↦ ↑17↓

139
Hot Coffee
Skill: Medium
←15↦ ↑19↓

140
Toast
Skill: Easy
←15↦ ↑15↓

141
Breakfast Sausage
Skill: Easy
←20↦ ↑13↓

In the Kitchen

KEY

CROSS STITCH

Use two strands

⊠	DMC-04
●	DMC-310
◀	DMC-317
✿	DMC-444
≈	DMC-727
△	DMC-828
◈	DMC-947
♥	DMC-957
//	DMC-959
◇	DMC-964
✳	DMC-995
▽	DMC-3843
∿	DMC-3845
▶▶	DMC-3846
○	DMC-White

BACKSTITCH

Use two strands

DMC-310

142
Teacup
Skill: Easy
←17→ ↑11↓

143
Teapot
Skill: Easy
←22→ ↑13↓

144
Braising Skillet
Skill: Medium
←23→ ↑11↓

145
Stovetop and Oven
Skill: Advanced
←19→ ↑22↓

146
Hand Mixer
Skill: Medium
←18→ ↑21↓

CROSS STITCH

Use two strands

 DMC-03

DMC-04

DMC-310

DMC-435

DMC-666

DMC-738

DMC-741

DMC-746

DMC-747

DMC-798

DMC-828

DMC-947

DMC-957

DMC-964

DMC-995

DMC-3845

DMC-3846

DMC-White

BACKSTITCH

Use two strands

DMC-310

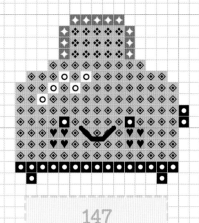

147
Toaster
Skill: Medium
←16→   ↑15↓

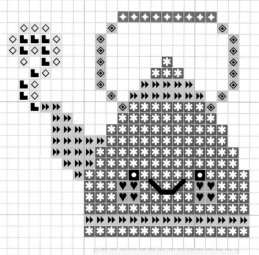

148
Kettle
Skill: Advanced
←22→   ↑20↓

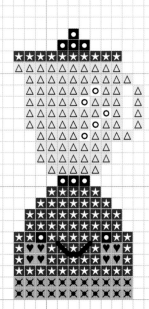

149
Oven Mitt
Skill: Medium
←17→   ↑17↓

150
Blender
Skill: Advanced
←12→   ↑24↓

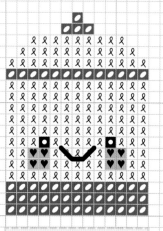

151
Cookie Jar
Skill: Easy
←13→   ↑18↓

DMC-03

DMC-04

DMC-310

DMC-435

DMC-437

DMC-702

DMC-704

DMC-731

DMC-734

DMC-740

DMC-741

DMC-957

DMC-964

DMC-White

BACKSTITCH

Use two strands

DMC-310

152
Kitchen Scale
Skill: Medium
←13→   ↑15↓

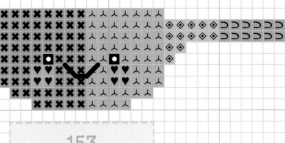

153
Saucepan
Skill: Easy
←26→   ↑9↓

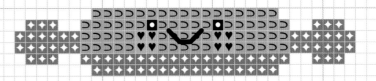

154
Rolling Pin
Skill: Easy
←31→   ↑6↓

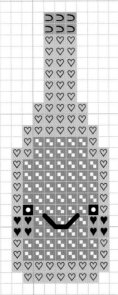

155
Olive Oil
Skill: Medium
←9→   ↑24↓

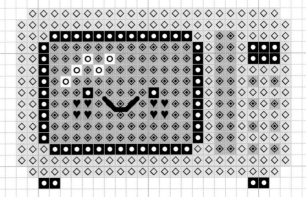

156
Microwave
Skill: Medium
←25→   ↑16↓

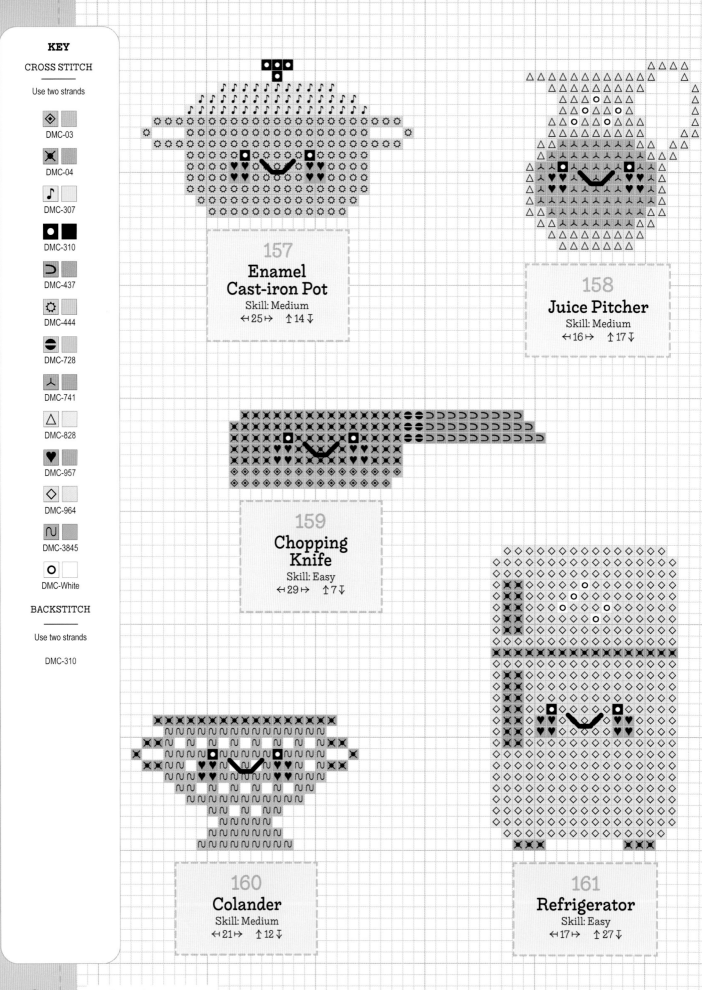

KEY

CROSS STITCH

Use two strands

◈	DMC-03
✖	DMC-04
♪	DMC-307
■	DMC-310
◗	DMC-437
✿	DMC-444
⬤	DMC-728
⊥	DMC-741
△	DMC-828
♥	DMC-957
◇	DMC-964
∿	DMC-3845
○	DMC-White

BACKSTITCH

Use two strands

DMC-310

157
**Enamel
Cast-iron Pot**
Skill: Medium
←25→ ↑14↓

158
Juice Pitcher
Skill: Medium
←16→ ↑17↓

159
**Chopping
Knife**
Skill: Easy
←29→ ↑7↓

160
Colander
Skill: Medium
←21→ ↑12↓

161
Refrigerator
Skill: Easy
←17→ ↑27↓

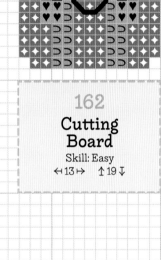

162
Cutting Board
Skill: Easy
←13↦ ↑19↓

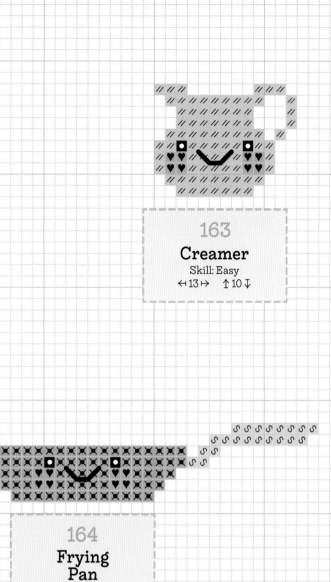

163
Creamer
Skill: Easy
←13↦ ↑10↓

164
Frying Pan
Skill: Easy
←31↦ ↑7↓

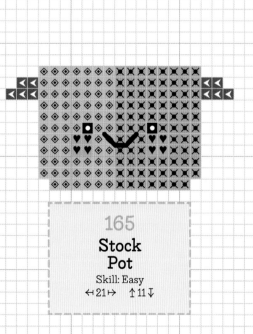

165
Stock Pot
Skill: Easy
←21↦ ↑11↓

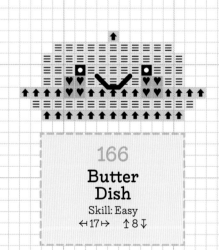

166
Butter Dish
Skill: Easy
←17↦ ↑8↓

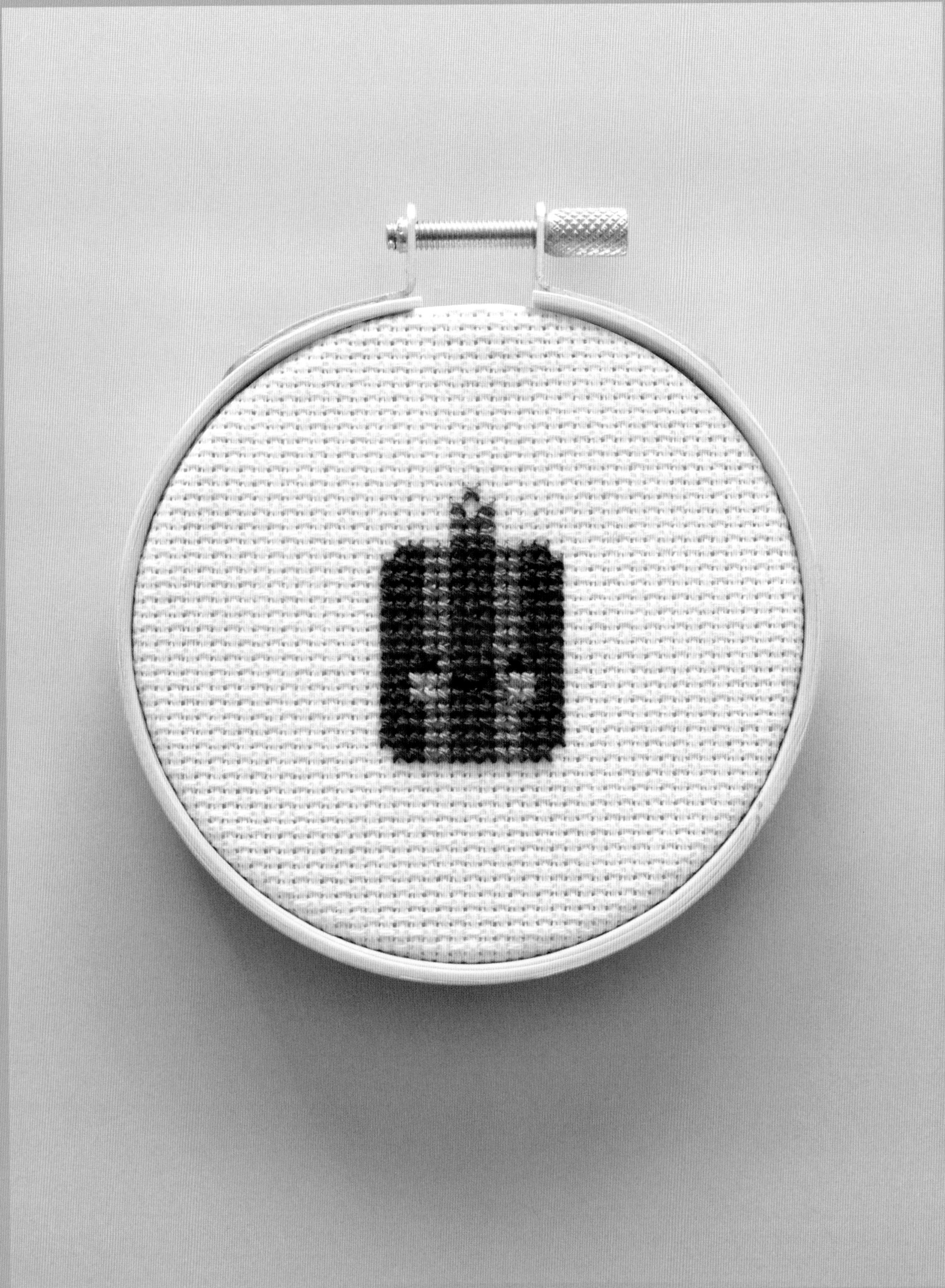

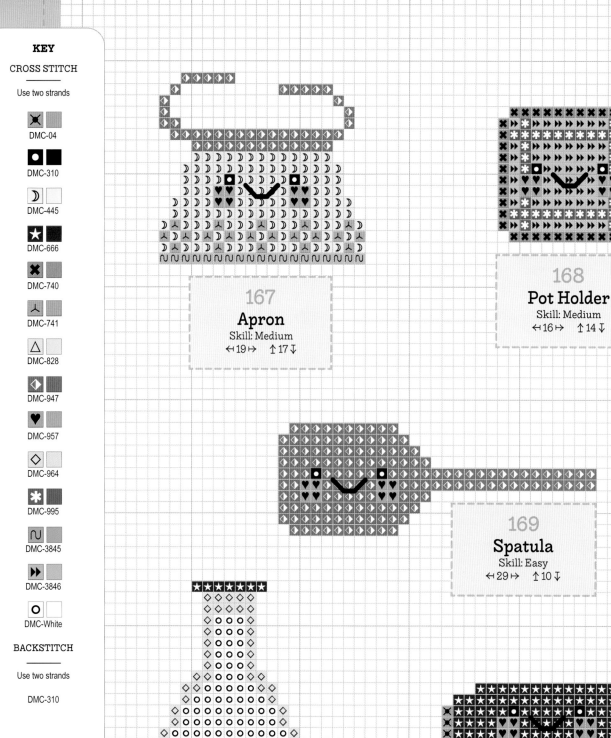

KEY

CROSS STITCH

Use two strands

DMC-04

DMC-310

DMC-445

DMC-666

DMC-740

DMC-741

DMC-828

DMC-947

DMC-957

DMC-964

DMC-995

DMC-3845

DMC-3846

DMC-White

BACKSTITCH

Use two strands

DMC-310

167
Apron
Skill: Medium
←19→ ↑17↓

168
Pot Holder
Skill: Medium
←16→ ↑14↓

169
Spatula
Skill: Easy
←29→ ↑10↓

170
Milk Bottle
Skill: Medium
←13→ ↑23↓

171
Stand Mixer
Skill: Medium
←26→ ↑19↓

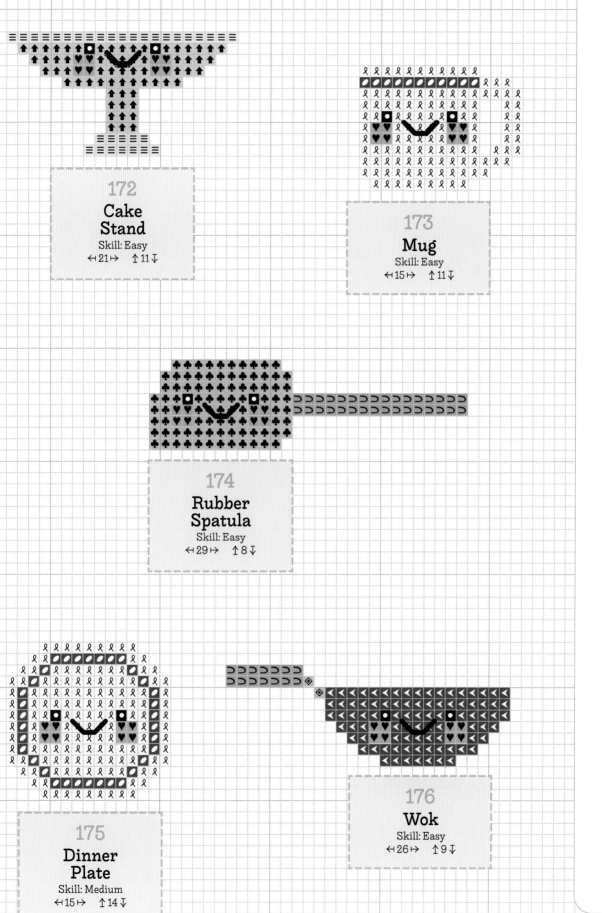

KEY

CROSS STITCH

Use two strands

DMC-03

DMC-310

DMC-317

DMC-437

DMC-746

DMC-798

DMC-906

DMC-954

DMC-955

DMC-957

BACKSTITCH

Use two strands

DMC-310

172
Cake Stand
Skill: Easy
←21↦ ↑11↓

173
Mug
Skill: Easy
←15↦ ↑11↓

174
Rubber Spatula
Skill: Easy
←29↦ ↑8↓

175
Dinner Plate
Skill: Medium
←15↦ ↑14↓

176
Wok
Skill: Easy
←26↦ ↑9↓

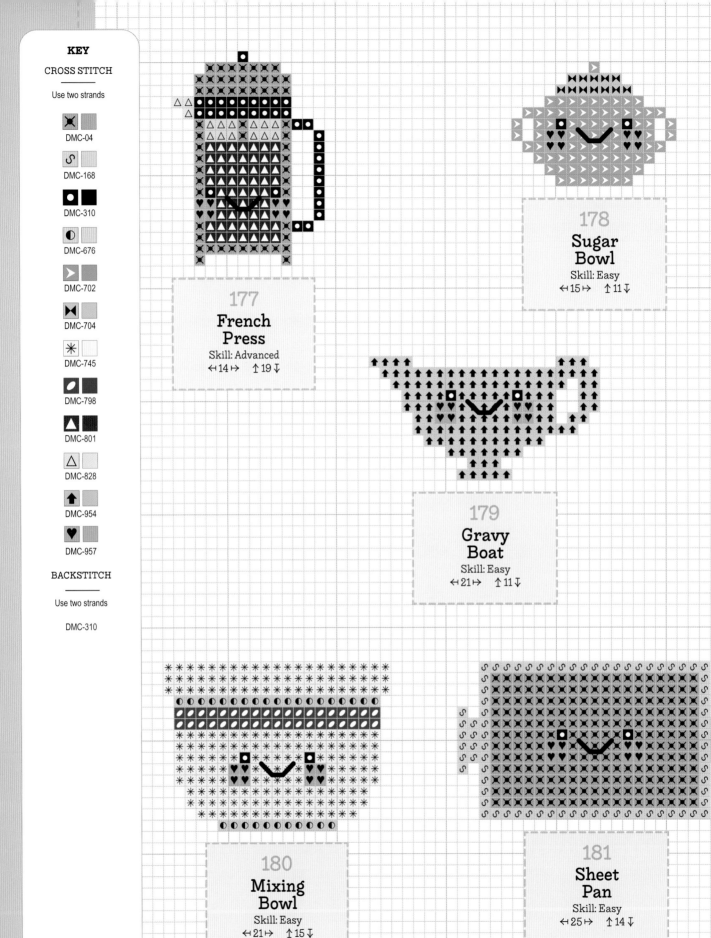

KEY

CROSS STITCH

Use two strands

DMC-04
DMC-168
DMC-310
DMC-676
DMC-702
DMC-704
DMC-745
DMC-798
DMC-801
DMC-828
DMC-954
DMC-957

BACKSTITCH

Use two strands

DMC-310

177
**French
Press**
Skill: Advanced
←14→ ↑19↓

178
**Sugar
Bowl**
Skill: Easy
←15→ ↑11↓

179
**Gravy
Boat**
Skill: Easy
←21→ ↑11↓

180
**Mixing
Bowl**
Skill: Easy
←21→ ↑15↓

181
**Sheet
Pan**
Skill: Easy
←25→ ↑14↓

Adorable Animals

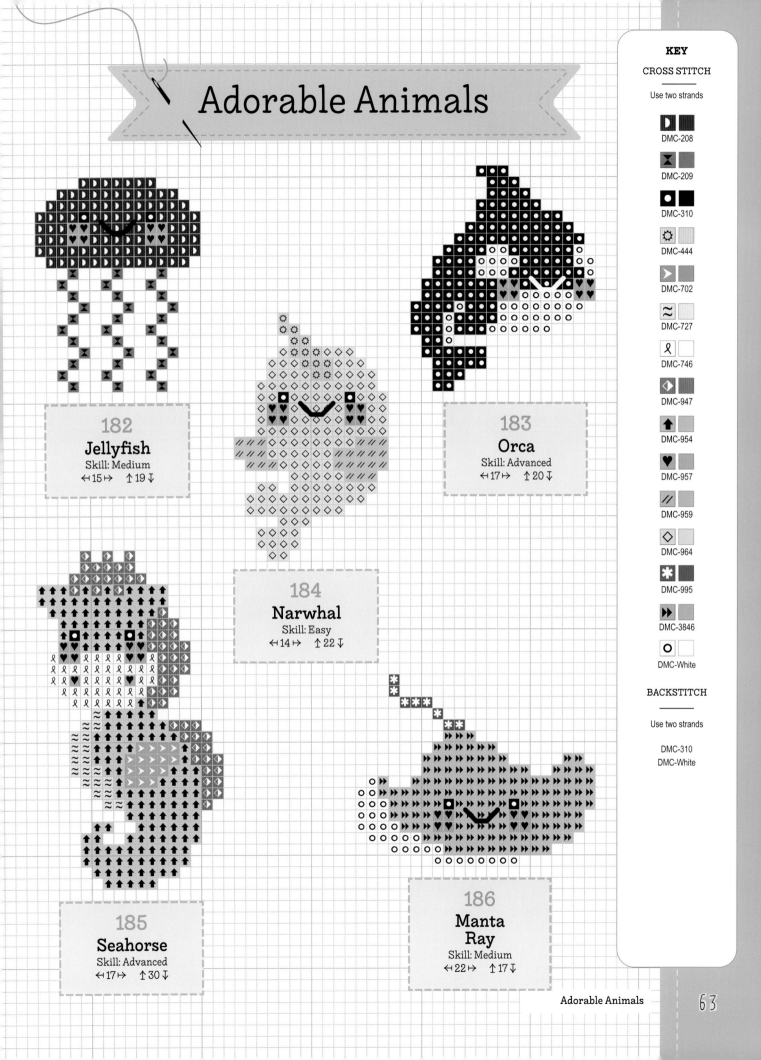

KEY

CROSS STITCH

Use two strands

DMC-208
DMC-209
DMC-310
DMC-444
DMC-702
DMC-727
DMC-746
DMC-947
DMC-954
DMC-957
DMC-959
DMC-964
DMC-995
DMC-3846
DMC-White

BACKSTITCH

Use two strands

DMC-310
DMC-White

182
Jellyfish
Skill: Medium
←15→   ↑19↓

183
Orca
Skill: Advanced
←17→   ↑20↓

184
Narwhal
Skill: Easy
←14→   ↑22↓

185
Seahorse
Skill: Advanced
←17→   ↑30↓

186
Manta Ray
Skill: Medium
←22→   ↑17↓

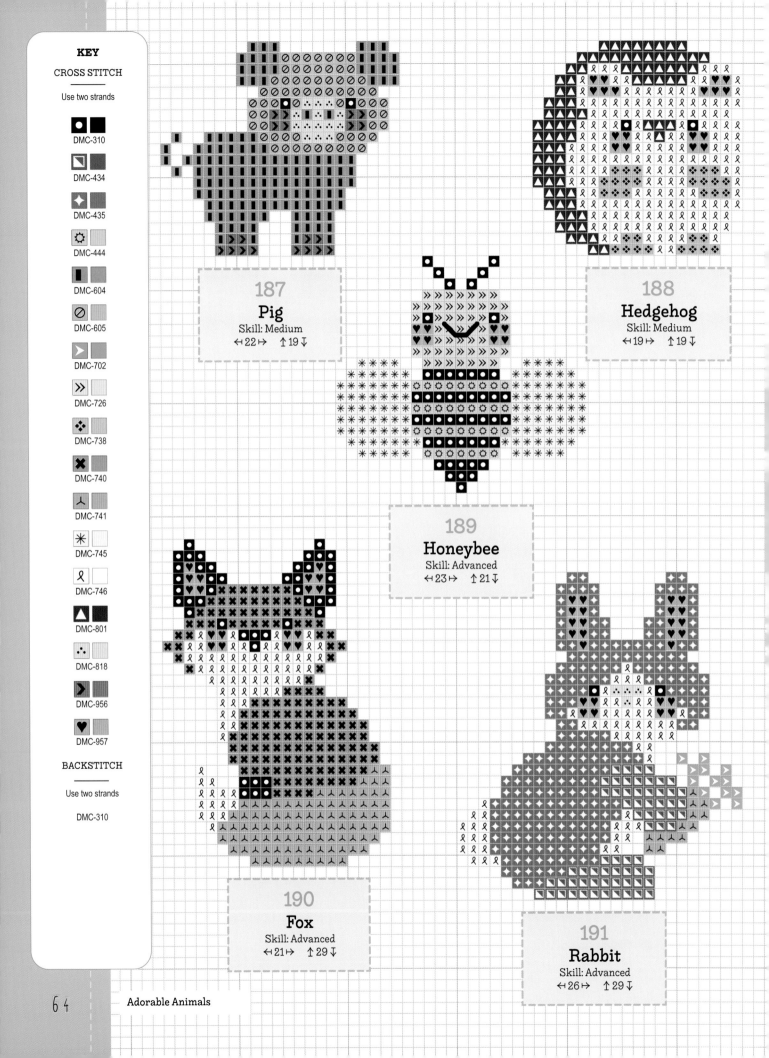

KEY

CROSS STITCH

Use two strands

⬤ ⬛	DMC-310
◨	DMC-434
◆	DMC-435
✿	DMC-444
▮	DMC-604
⊘	DMC-605
▶	DMC-702
»	DMC-726
❖	DMC-738
✖	DMC-740
⼈	DMC-741
✳	DMC-745
⼂	DMC-746
▲ ◣	DMC-801
∴	DMC-818
▶	DMC-956
♥	DMC-957

BACKSTITCH

Use two strands

DMC-310

187
Pig
Skill: Medium
←22→ ↑19↓

188
Hedgehog
Skill: Medium
←19→ ↑19↓

189
Honeybee
Skill: Advanced
←23→ ↑21↓

190
Fox
Skill: Advanced
←21→ ↑29↓

191
Rabbit
Skill: Advanced
←26→ ↑29↓

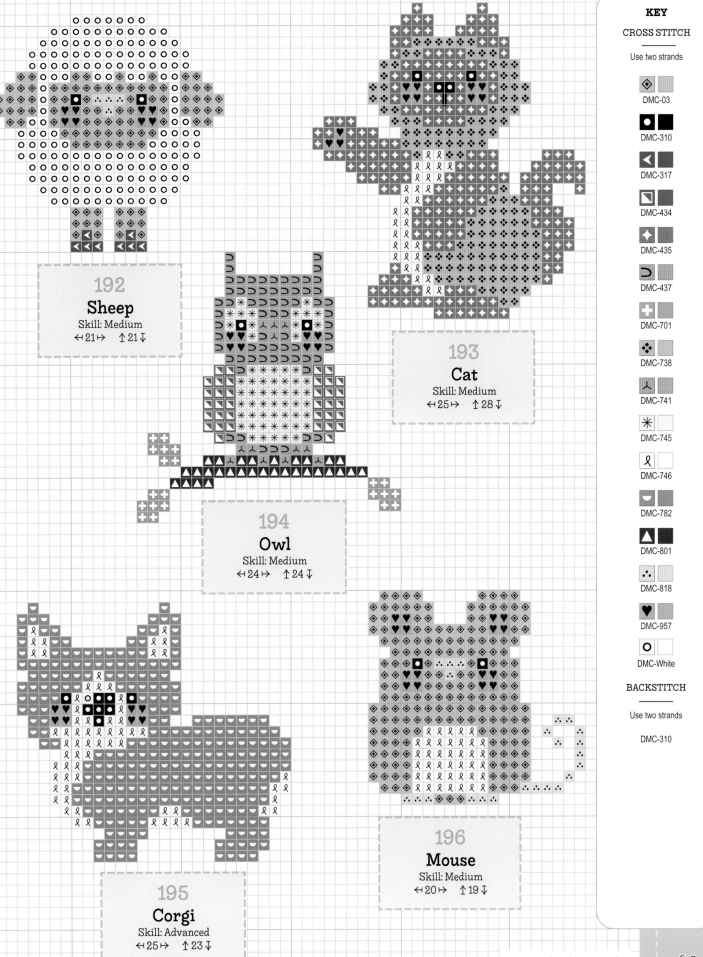

KEY

CROSS STITCH

Use two strands

◈	DMC-03
● ■	DMC-310
◀	DMC-317
◥	DMC-434
◆	DMC-435
⊃	DMC-437
✚	DMC-701
❖	DMC-738
⊿	DMC-741
✳	DMC-745
℔	DMC-746
⌓	DMC-782
▲	DMC-801
∴	DMC-818
♥	DMC-957
○	DMC-White

BACKSTITCH

Use two strands

DMC-310

192

Sheep

Skill: Medium

←21↦ ↥21↓

193

Cat

Skill: Medium

←25↦ ↥28↓

194

Owl

Skill: Medium

←24↦ ↥24↓

195

Corgi

Skill: Advanced

←25↦ ↥23↓

196

Mouse

Skill: Medium

←20↦ ↥19↓

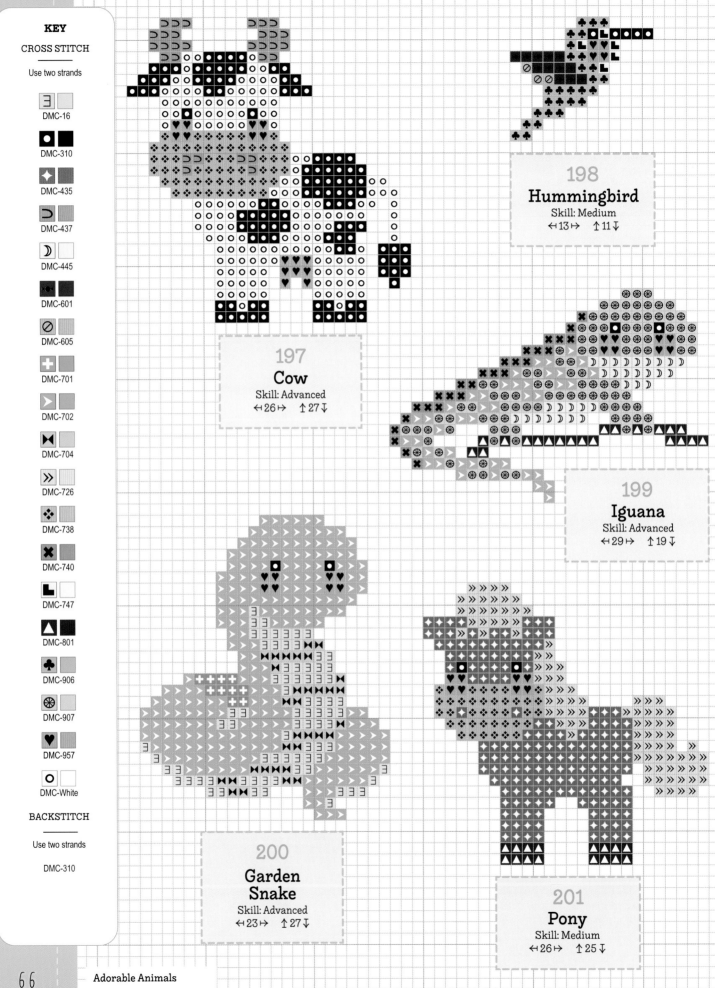

KEY

CROSS STITCH

Use two strands

∃ DMC-16
● DMC-310
◆ DMC-435
⊃ DMC-437
☽ DMC-445
◀▶ DMC-601
⊘ DMC-605
✚ DMC-701
▶ DMC-702
◀▶ DMC-704
≫ DMC-726
❖ DMC-738
✖ DMC-740
◣ DMC-747
▲ DMC-801
♣ DMC-906
✺ DMC-907
♥ DMC-957
○ DMC-White

BACKSTITCH

Use two strands

DMC-310

198
Hummingbird
Skill: Medium
←13→ ↑11↓

197
Cow
Skill: Advanced
←26→ ↑27↓

199
Iguana
Skill: Advanced
←29→ ↑19↓

200
Garden Snake
Skill: Advanced
←23→ ↑27↓

201
Pony
Skill: Medium
←26→ ↑25↓

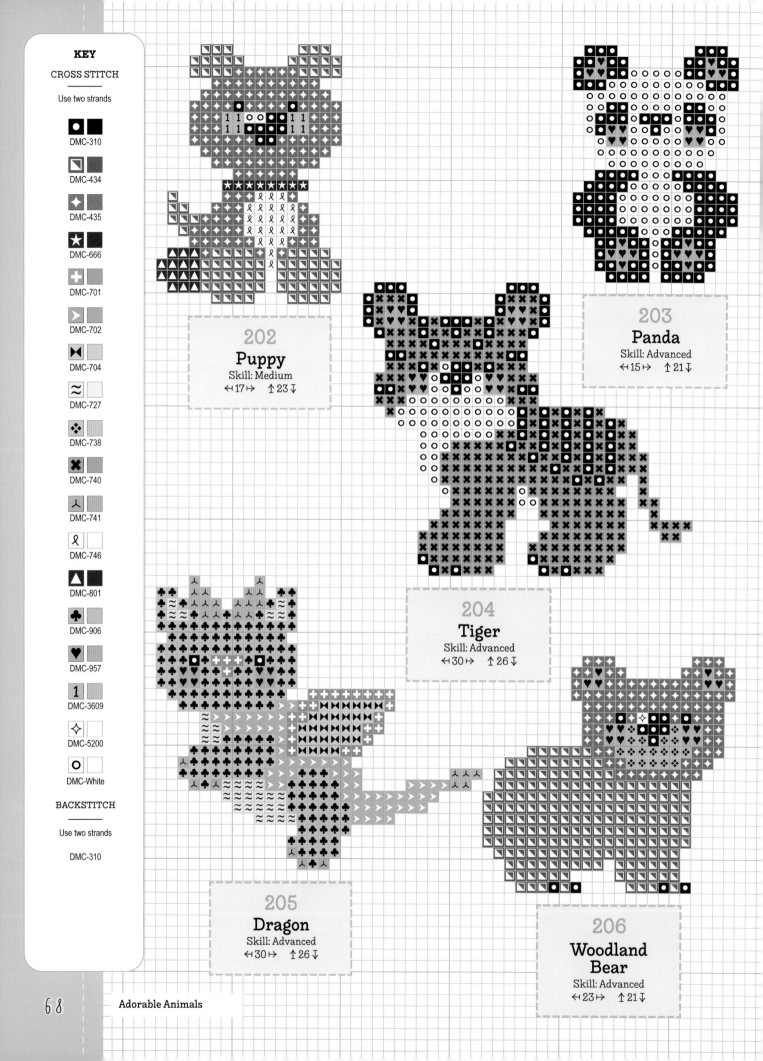

KEY

CROSS STITCH

Use two strands

● ■	DMC-310	
◥ ■	DMC-434	
✦ ■	DMC-435	
★ ■	DMC-666	
✚ ■	DMC-701	
▶ ■	DMC-702	
◄► ■	DMC-704	
≈ ■	DMC-727	
❖ ■	DMC-738	
✖ ■	DMC-740	
⅄ ■	DMC-741	
₰ □	DMC-746	
△ ■	DMC-801	
♣ ■	DMC-906	
♥ ■	DMC-957	
1 ■	DMC-3609	
✧ □	DMC-5200	
○ □	DMC-White	

BACKSTITCH

Use two strands

DMC-310

202

Puppy

Skill: Medium

←17→ ↑23↓

203

Panda

Skill: Advanced

←15→ ↑21↓

204

Tiger

Skill: Advanced

←30→ ↑26↓

205

Dragon

Skill: Advanced

←30→ ↑26↓

206

Woodland Bear

Skill: Advanced

←23→ ↑21↓

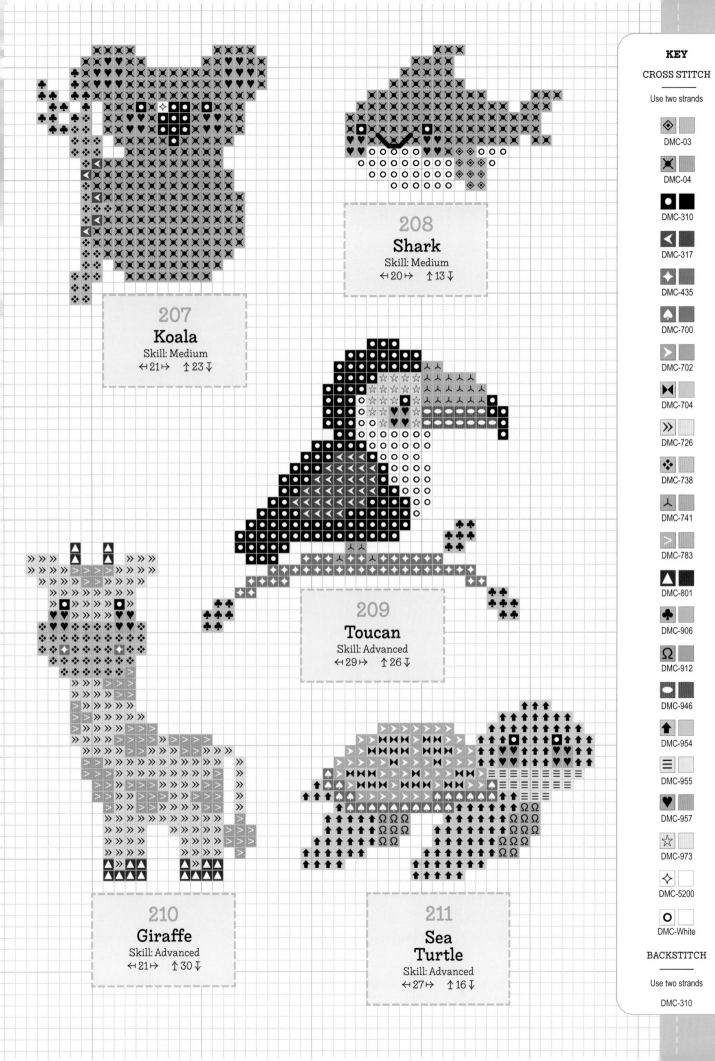

207
Koala
Skill: Medium
←21↦ ↑23↓

208
Shark
Skill: Medium
←20↦ ↑13↓

209
Toucan
Skill: Advanced
←29↦ ↑26↓

210
Giraffe
Skill: Advanced
←21↦ ↑30↓

211
Sea Turtle
Skill: Advanced
←27↦ ↑16↓

KEY

CROSS STITCH

Use two strands

DMC-03
DMC-04
DMC-310
DMC-317
DMC-435
DMC-700
DMC-702
DMC-704
DMC-726
DMC-738
DMC-741
DMC-783
DMC-801
DMC-906
DMC-912
DMC-946
DMC-954
DMC-955
DMC-957
DMC-973
DMC-5200
DMC-White

BACKSTITCH

Use two strands

DMC-310

KEY

CROSS STITCH

Use two strands

DMC-16	
DMC-310	
DMC-435	
DMC-437	
DMC-700	
DMC-701	
DMC-702	
DMC-726	
DMC-728	
DMC-740	
DMC-741	
DMC-746	
DMC-782	
DMC-801	
DMC-906	
DMC-907	
DMC-947	
DMC-957	
DMC-White	

BACKSTITCH

Use two strands

DMC-310

212
Tortoise
Skill: Medium
←27→ ↑16↓

213
Octopus
Skill: Medium
←24→ ↑23↓

214
Gecko
Skill: Medium
←25→ ↑14↓

215
Guinea Pig
Skill: Medium
←19→ ↑15↓

216
Lion
Skill: Advanced
←32→ ↑29↓

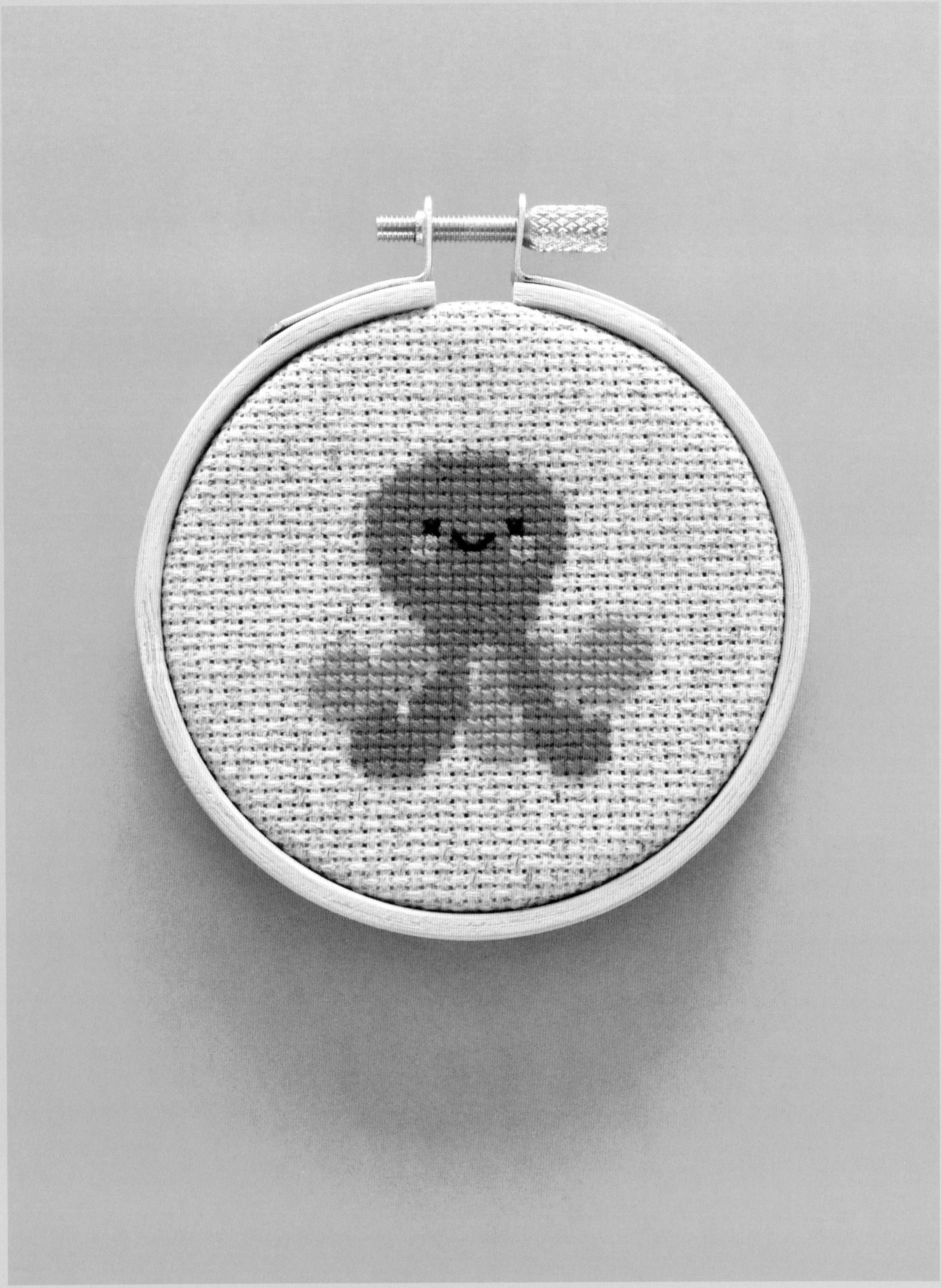

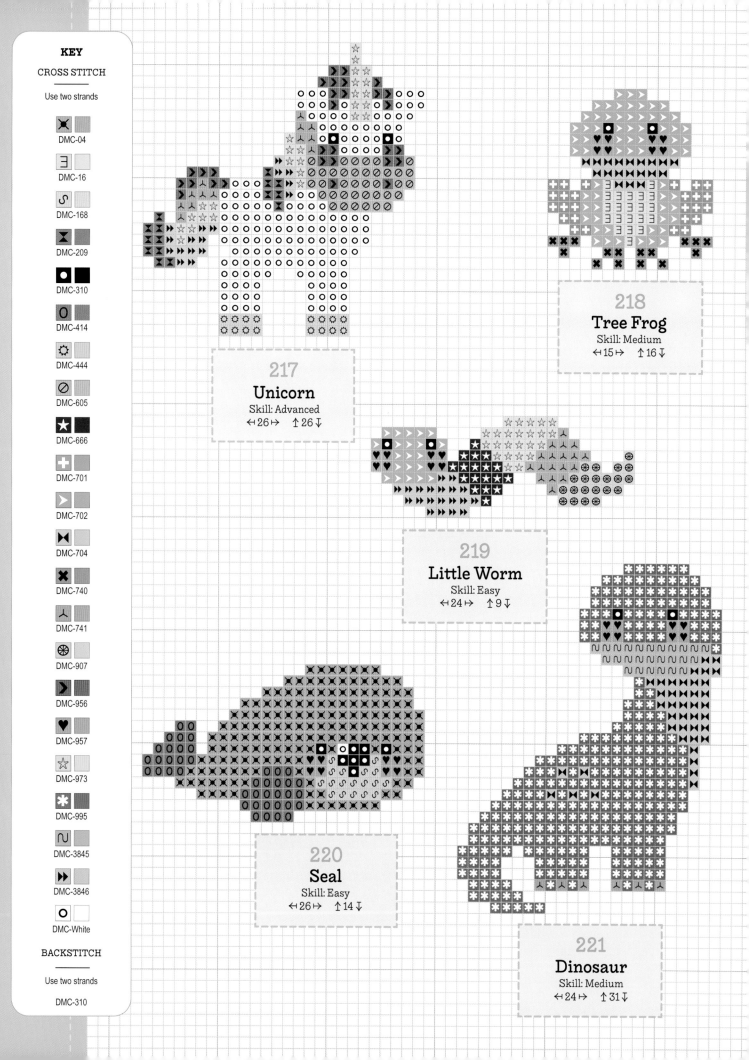

KEY

CROSS STITCH

Use two strands

DMC-04
DMC-16
DMC-168
DMC-209
DMC-310
DMC-414
DMC-444
DMC-605
DMC-666
DMC-701
DMC-702
DMC-704
DMC-740
DMC-741
DMC-907
DMC-956
DMC-957
DMC-973
DMC-995
DMC-3845
DMC-3846
DMC-White

BACKSTITCH

Use two strands

DMC-310

217
Unicorn
Skill: Advanced
←26→ ↑26↓

218
Tree Frog
Skill: Medium
←15→ ↑16↓

219
Little Worm
Skill: Easy
←24→ ↑9↓

220
Seal
Skill: Easy
←26→ ↑14↓

221
Dinosaur
Skill: Medium
←24→ ↑31↓

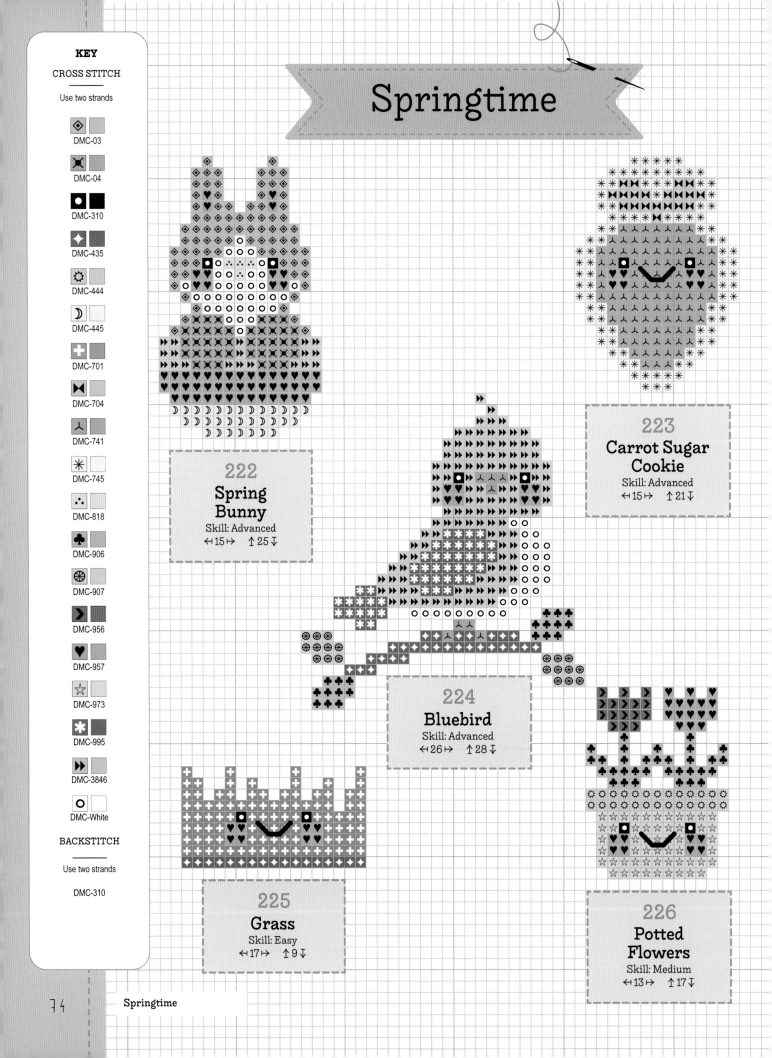

KEY

CROSS STITCH

Use two strands

◈	DMC-03
✖	DMC-04
◖	DMC-310
✦	DMC-435
✿	DMC-444
☽	DMC-445
✚	DMC-701
▶◀	DMC-704
⊥	DMC-741
✳	DMC-745
∴	DMC-818
♣	DMC-906
✺	DMC-907
▶	DMC-956
♥	DMC-957
☆	DMC-973
✳	DMC-995
▶▶	DMC-3846
○	DMC-White

BACKSTITCH

Use two strands

DMC-310

Springtime

222
Spring Bunny
Skill: Advanced
←15→ ↑25↓

223
Carrot Sugar Cookie
Skill: Advanced
←15→ ↑21↓

224
Bluebird
Skill: Advanced
←26→ ↑28↓

225
Grass
Skill: Easy
←17→ ↑9↓

226
Potted Flowers
Skill: Medium
←13→ ↑17↓

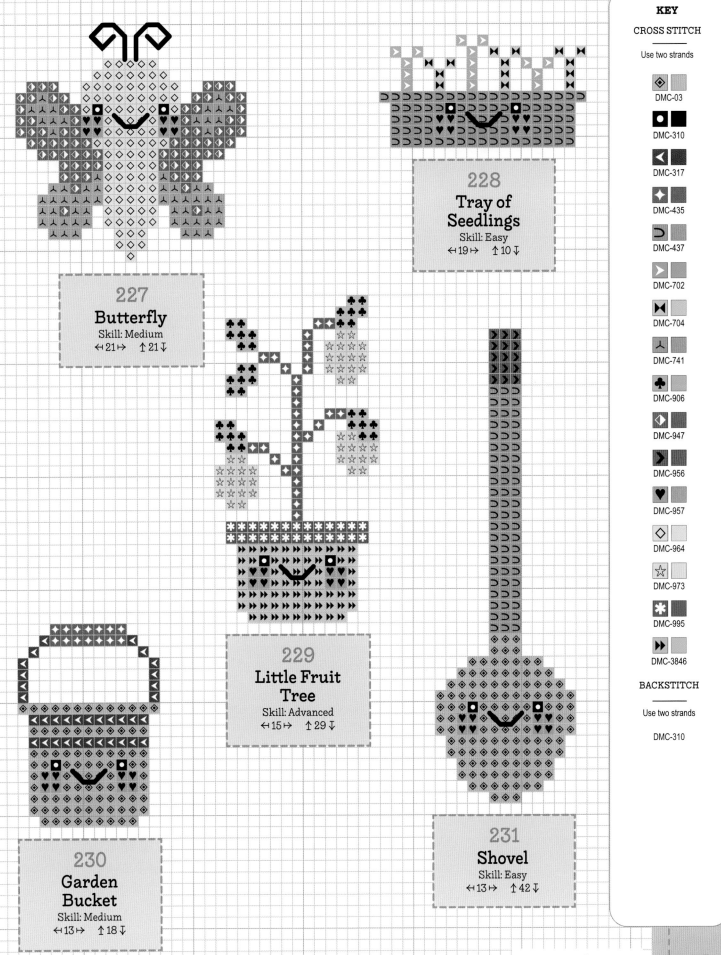

KEY

CROSS STITCH

Use two strands

◇	DMC-03
◉	DMC-310
◀	DMC-317
✦	DMC-435
Ɔ	DMC-437
▷	DMC-702
▶◀	DMC-704
人	DMC-741
♣	DMC-906
◈	DMC-947
▶	DMC-956
♥	DMC-957
◇	DMC-964
☆	DMC-973
✳	DMC-995
▶▶	DMC-3846

BACKSTITCH

Use two strands

DMC-310

227
Butterfly
Skill: Medium
←21↦ ↑21↓

228
Tray of Seedlings
Skill: Easy
←19↦ ↑10↓

229
Little Fruit Tree
Skill: Advanced
←15↦ ↑29↓

230
Garden Bucket
Skill: Medium
←13↦ ↑18↓

231
Shovel
Skill: Easy
←13↦ ↑42↓

KEY

CROSS STITCH

Use two strands

 DMC-03

 DMC-310

 DMC-435

 DMC-437

 DMC-444

 DMC-445

 DMC-704

 DMC-727

 DMC-741

 DMC-906

 DMC-956

 DMC-957

 DMC-964

 DMC-995

 DMC-3846

DMC-White

BACKSTITCH

Use two strands

DMC-310

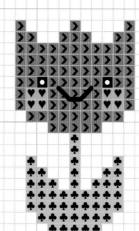

232
Tulip
Skill: Medium
←11→   ↑19↓

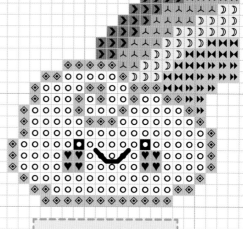

233
Rainbow Cloud
Skill: Advanced
←21→   ↑22↓

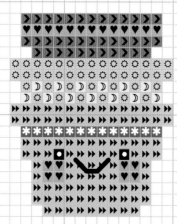

234
Spotted Egg
Skill: Medium
←13→   ↑14↓

235
Flower Pots
Skill: Advanced
←15→   ↑18↓

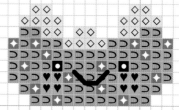

236
Bird's Nest
Skill: Medium
←15→   ↑9↓

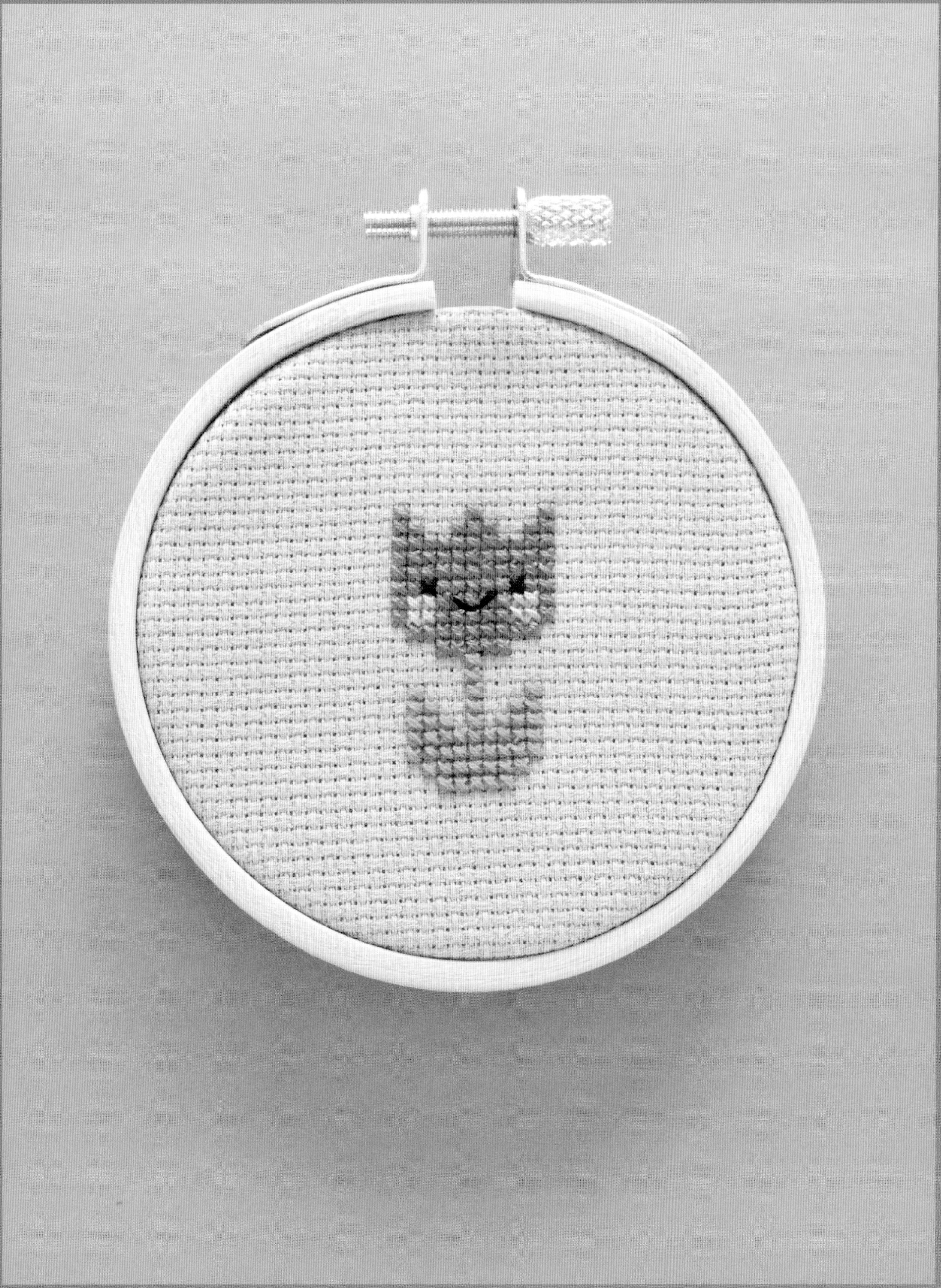

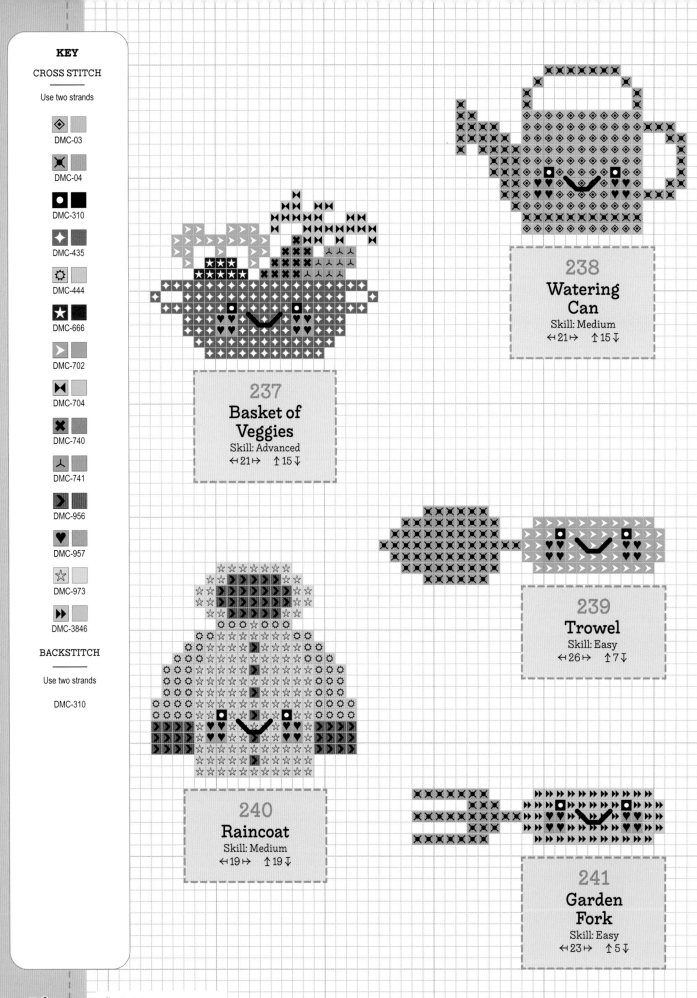

KEY

CROSS STITCH

Use two strands

◈	DMC-03
✖	DMC-04
◘	DMC-310
✦	DMC-435
✿	DMC-444
★	DMC-666
▶	DMC-702
◀▶	DMC-704
✖	DMC-740
人	DMC-741
▶	DMC-956
♥	DMC-957
☆	DMC-973
▶▶	DMC-3846

BACKSTITCH

Use two strands

DMC-310

238
Watering Can
Skill: Medium
←21→ ↑15↓

237
Basket of Veggies
Skill: Advanced
←21→ ↑15↓

239
Trowel
Skill: Easy
←26→ ↑7↓

240
Raincoat
Skill: Medium
←19→ ↑19↓

241
Garden Fork
Skill: Easy
←23→ ↑5↓

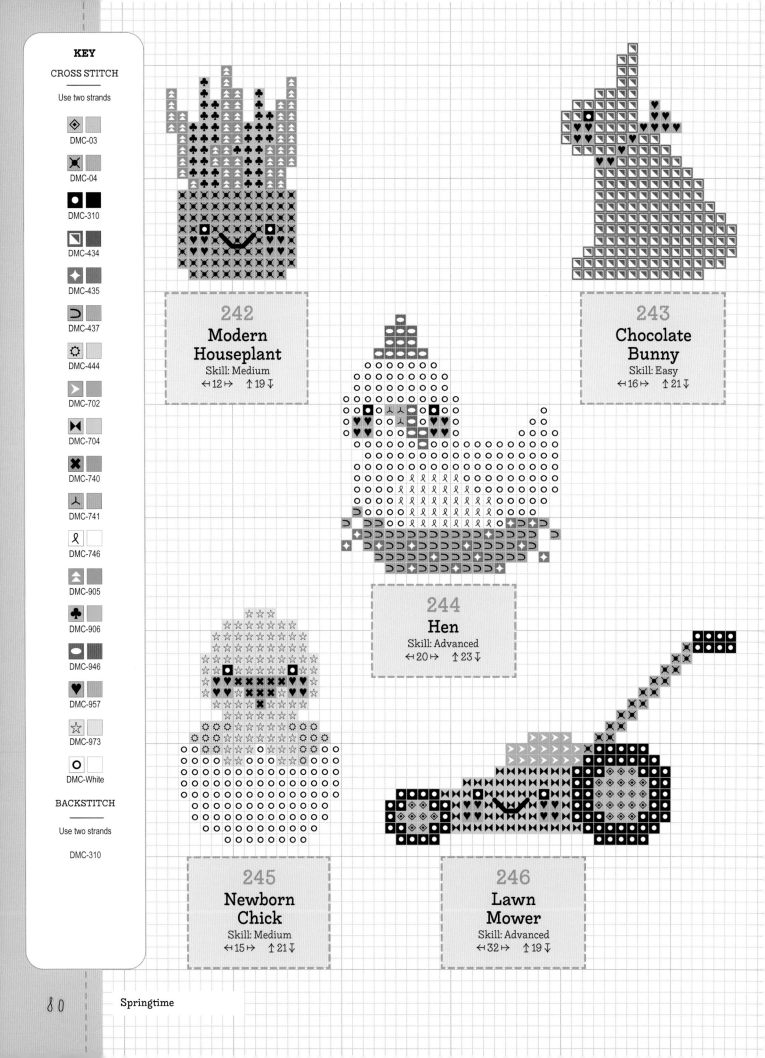

KEY

CROSS STITCH

Use two strands

DMC-03
DMC-04
DMC-310
DMC-434
DMC-435
DMC-437
DMC-444
DMC-702
DMC-704
DMC-740
DMC-741
DMC-746
DMC-905
DMC-906
DMC-946
DMC-957
DMC-973
DMC-White

BACKSTITCH

Use two strands

DMC-310

242
Modern Houseplant
Skill: Medium
←12→   ↑19↓

243
Chocolate Bunny
Skill: Easy
←16→   ↑21↓

244
Hen
Skill: Advanced
←20→   ↑23↓

245
Newborn Chick
Skill: Medium
←15→   ↑21↓

246
Lawn Mower
Skill: Advanced
←32→   ↑19↓

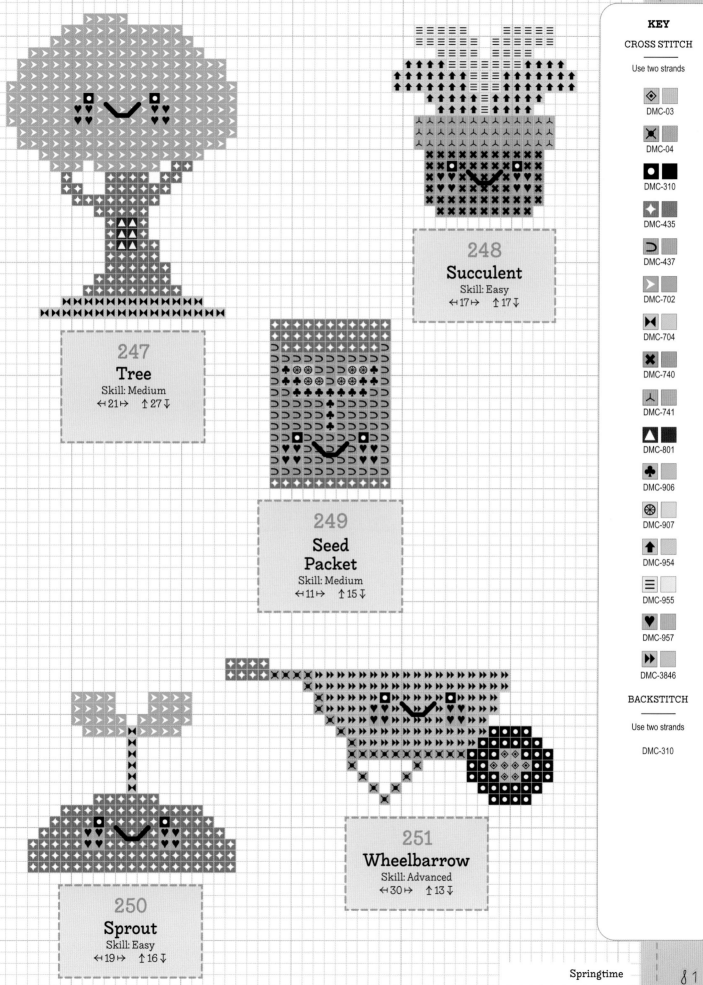

247
Tree
Skill: Medium
←21→ ↑27↓

248
Succulent
Skill: Easy
←17→ ↑17↓

249
Seed Packet
Skill: Medium
←11→ ↑15↓

250
Sprout
Skill: Easy
←19→ ↑16↓

251
Wheelbarrow
Skill: Advanced
←30→ ↑13↓

KEY

CROSS STITCH

Use two strands

DMC-03

DMC-04

DMC-310

DMC-435

DMC-437

DMC-702

DMC-704

DMC-740

DMC-741

DMC-801

DMC-906

DMC-907

DMC-954

DMC-955

DMC-957

DMC-3846

BACKSTITCH

Use two strands

DMC-310

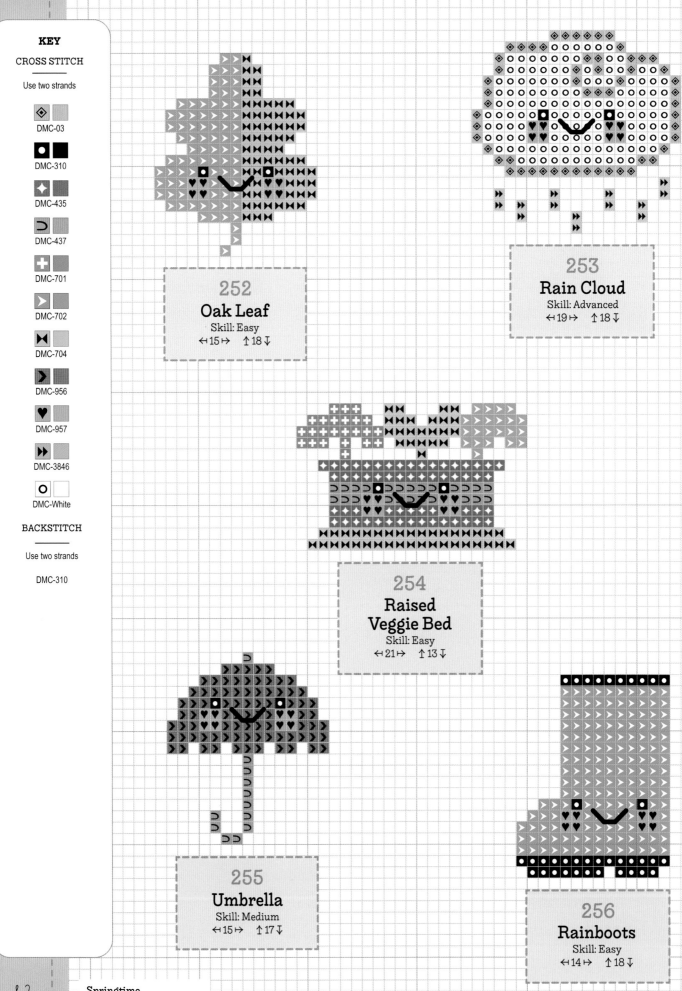

KEY

CROSS STITCH

Use two strands

DMC-03

DMC-310

DMC-435

DMC-437

DMC-701

DMC-702

DMC-704

DMC-956

DMC-957

DMC-3846

DMC-White

BACKSTITCH

Use two strands

DMC-310

252
Oak Leaf
Skill: Easy
←15↦   ↑18↓

253
Rain Cloud
Skill: Advanced
←19↦   ↑18↓

254
**Raised
Veggie Bed**
Skill: Easy
←21↦   ↑13↓

255
Umbrella
Skill: Medium
←15↦   ↑17↓

256
Rainboots
Skill: Easy
←14↦   ↑18↓

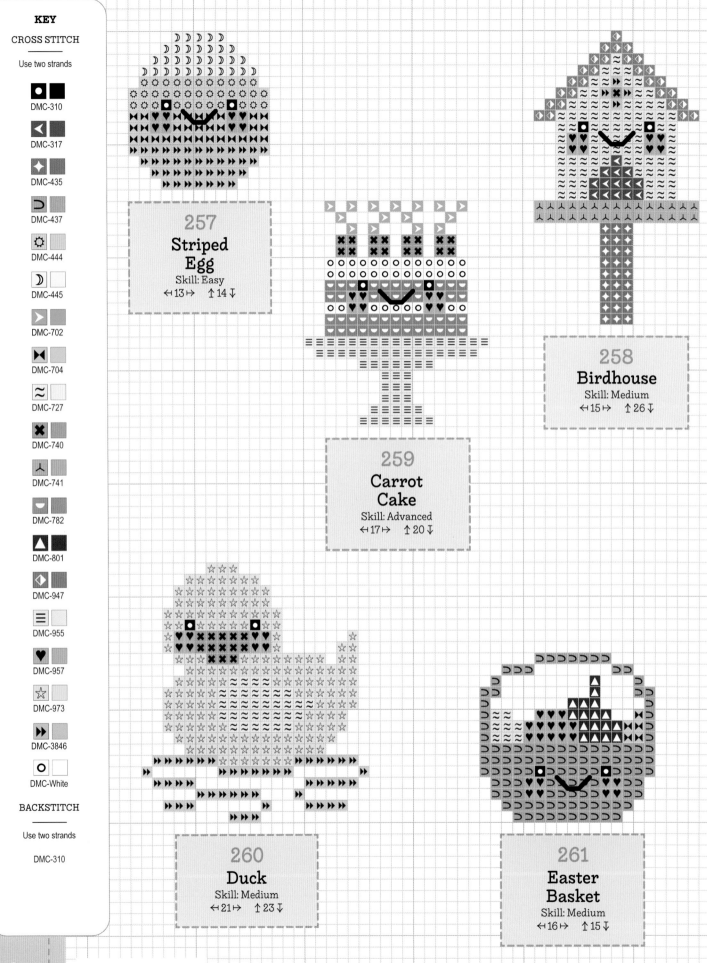

KEY

CROSS STITCH

Use two strands

DMC-310	
DMC-317	
DMC-435	
DMC-437	
DMC-444	
DMC-445	
DMC-702	
DMC-704	
DMC-727	
DMC-740	
DMC-741	
DMC-782	
DMC-801	
DMC-947	
DMC-955	
DMC-957	
DMC-973	
DMC-3846	
DMC-White	

BACKSTITCH

Use two strands

DMC-310

257
Striped Egg
Skill: Easy
←13↦ ↑14↓

259
Carrot Cake
Skill: Advanced
←17↦ ↑20↓

258
Birdhouse
Skill: Medium
←15↦ ↑26↓

260
Duck
Skill: Medium
←21↦ ↑23↓

261
Easter Basket
Skill: Medium
←16↦ ↑15↓

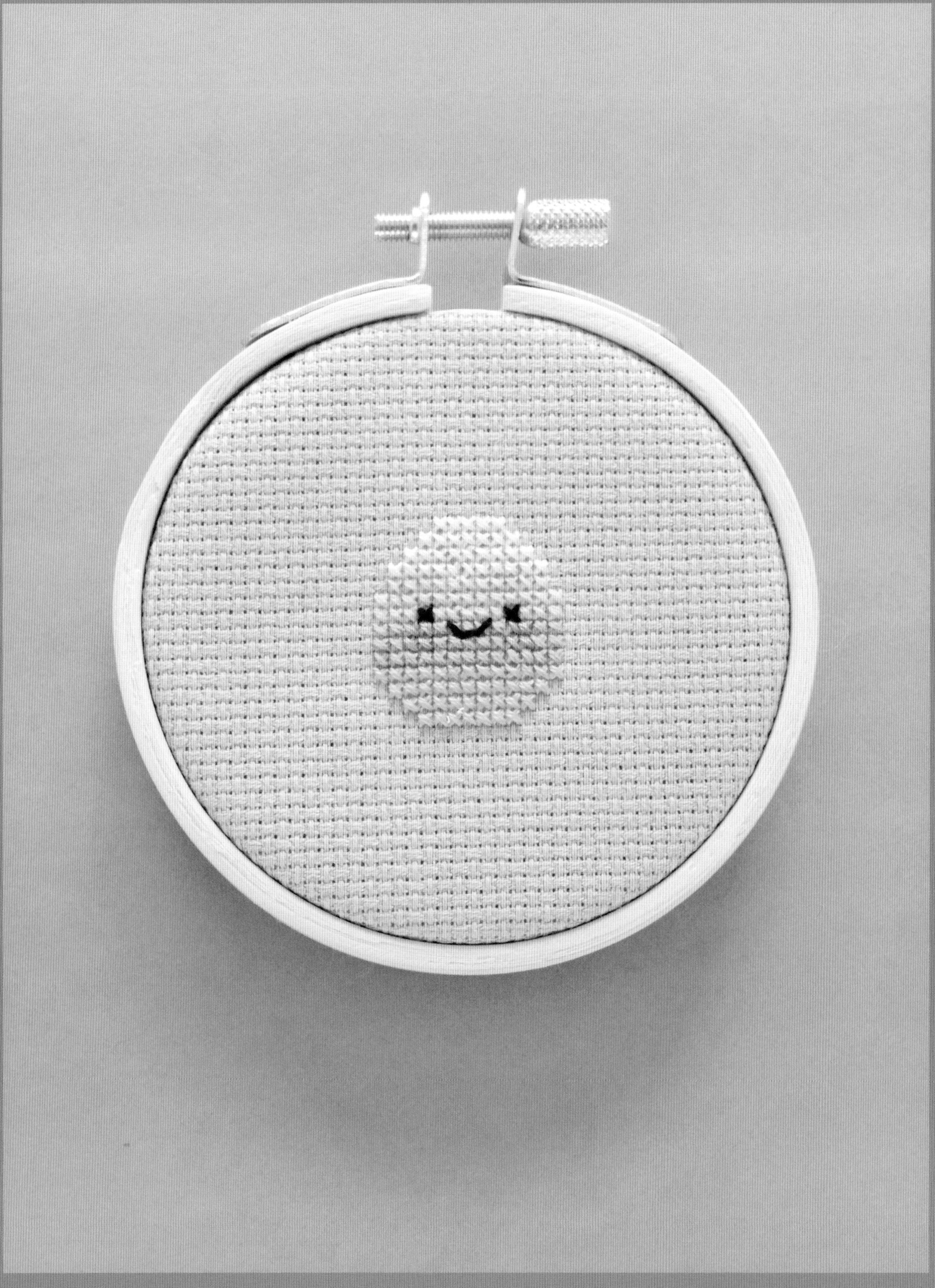

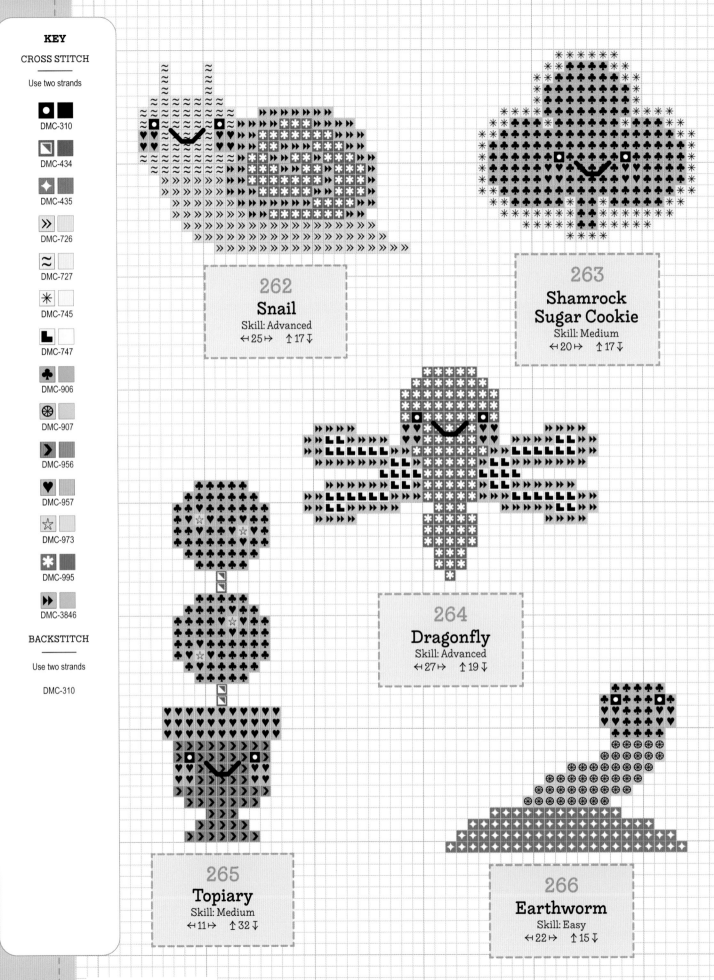

KEY

CROSS STITCH

Use two strands

DMC-310

DMC-434

DMC-435

DMC-726

DMC-727

DMC-745

DMC-747

DMC-906

DMC-907

DMC-956

DMC-957

DMC-973

DMC-995

DMC-3846

BACKSTITCH

Use two strands

DMC-310

262
Snail
Skill: Advanced
←25→ ↑17↓

263
**Shamrock
Sugar Cookie**
Skill: Medium
←20→ ↑17↓

264
Dragonfly
Skill: Advanced
←27→ ↑19↓

265
Topiary
Skill: Medium
←11→ ↑32↓

266
Earthworm
Skill: Easy
←22→ ↑15↓

Summer Fun

267
Starfish
Skill: Advanced
←21→ ↑21↓

268
Sunshine
Skill: Advanced
←17→ ↑17↓

269
Hot Air Ballon
Skill: Advanced
←13→ ↑20↓

270
Beach Hut
Skill: Medium
←17→ ↑19↓

271
Sailboat
Skill: Medium
←20→ ↑16↓

KEY

CROSS STITCH

Use two strands

 DMC-03

 DMC-04

 DMC-310

 DMC-317

 DMC-434

 DMC-437

 DMC-444

 DMC-666

 DMC-702

 DMC-746

 DMC-956

 DMC-957

 DMC-973

 DMC-3846

 DMC-White

BACKSTITCH

Use two strands

DMC-310

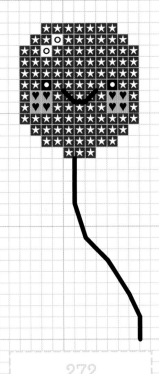

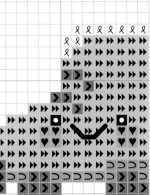

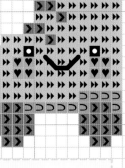

272
Balloon
Skill: Medium
←11↦ ↑28↓

273
Retro Radio
Skill: Medium
←18↦ ↑12↓

274
Rollerskates
Skill: Medium
←15↦ ↑17↓

275
Skateboard
Skill: Easy
←29↦ ↑7↓

276
Guitar
Skill: Advanced
←15↦ ↑28↓

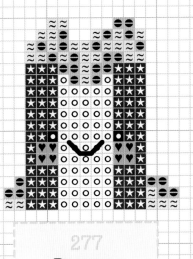

277
Popcorn
Skill: Advanced
←16↦ ↑17↓

KEY

CROSS STITCH

Use two strands

DMC-04

DMC-310

DMC-434

DMC-435

DMC-437

DMC-444

DMC-666

DMC-726

DMC-727

DMC-728

DMC-741

DMC-828

DMC-947

DMC-957

DMC-White

BACKSTITCH

Use two strands

DMC-310

278
Little Fish
Skill: Easy
←19↦ ↑12↓

279
Camper
Skill: Advanced
←22↦ ↑15↓

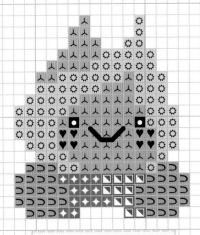

280
Camp Fire
Skill: Medium
←16↦ ↑18↓

281
Picnic Basket
Skill: Advanced
←17↦ ↑15↓

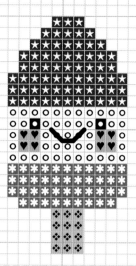

282
Rocket Pop
Skill: Easy
←11↦   ↑21↓

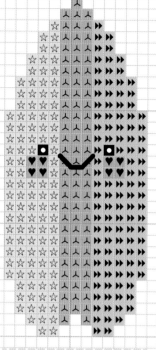

283
Surfboard
Skill: Easy
←13↦   ↑30↓

284
Sunblock
Skill: Medium
←9↦   ↑19↓

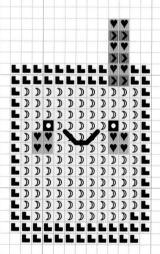

285
Lemonade
Skill: Medium
←13↦   ↑20↓

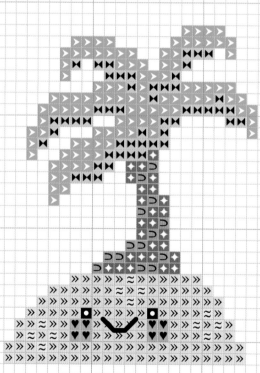

286
Little Island
Skill: Advanced
←23↦   ↑30↓

KEY

CROSS STITCH

Use two strands

DMC-310

DMC-666

DMC-702

DMC-726

DMC-728

DMC-783

DMC-798

DMC-818

DMC-947

DMC-957

DMC-973

DMC-3846

DMC-White

BACKSTITCH

Use two strands

DMC-310

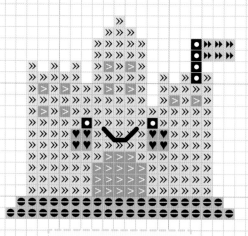

287
Crab
Skill: Medium
←21↦ ↑11↓

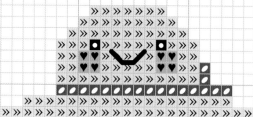

288
Sunhat
Skill: Easy
←23↦ ↑10↓

289
Castle
Skill: Medium
←21↦ ↑18↓

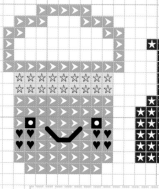

291
Shovel and Pail
Skill: Easy
←17↦ ↑15↓

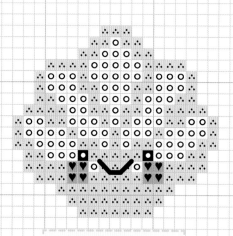

290
Seashell
Skill: Advanced
←19↦ ↑17↓

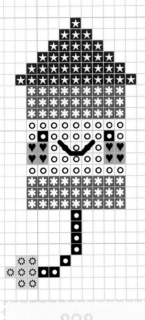

292
Fireworks
Skill: Medium
←12→ ↑24↓

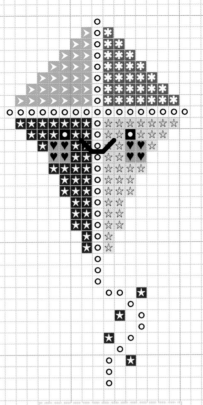

293
Kite
Skill: Advanced
←17→ ↑33↓

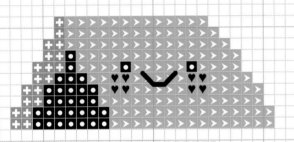

294
Tent
Skill: Easy
←24→ ↑10↓

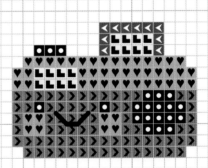

296
Camera
Skill: Advanced
←17→ ↑12↓

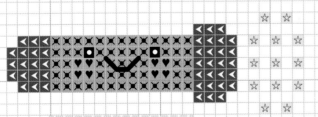

295
Flashlight
Skill: Advanced
←27→ ↑9↓

CROSS STITCH

Use two strands

DMC-04

DMC-310

DMC-317

DMC-444

DMC-666

DMC-701

DMC-702

DMC-747

DMC-956

DMC-957

DMC-973

DMC-995

DMC-White

BACKSTITCH

Use two strands

DMC-310

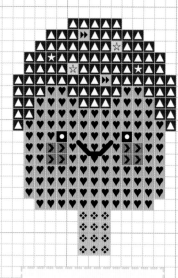

297

Fudge Pop

Skill: Advanced

←15→   ↑21↓

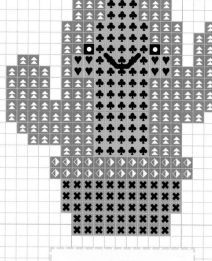

298

Cactus

Skill: Medium

←21→   ↑23↓

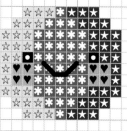

299

Beachball

Skill: Easy

←11→   ↑10↓

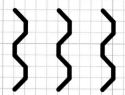

301

BBQ Grill

Skill: Medium

←17→   ↑22↓

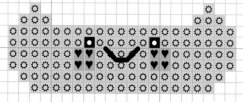

300

Canoe

Skill: Easy

←21→   ↑12↓

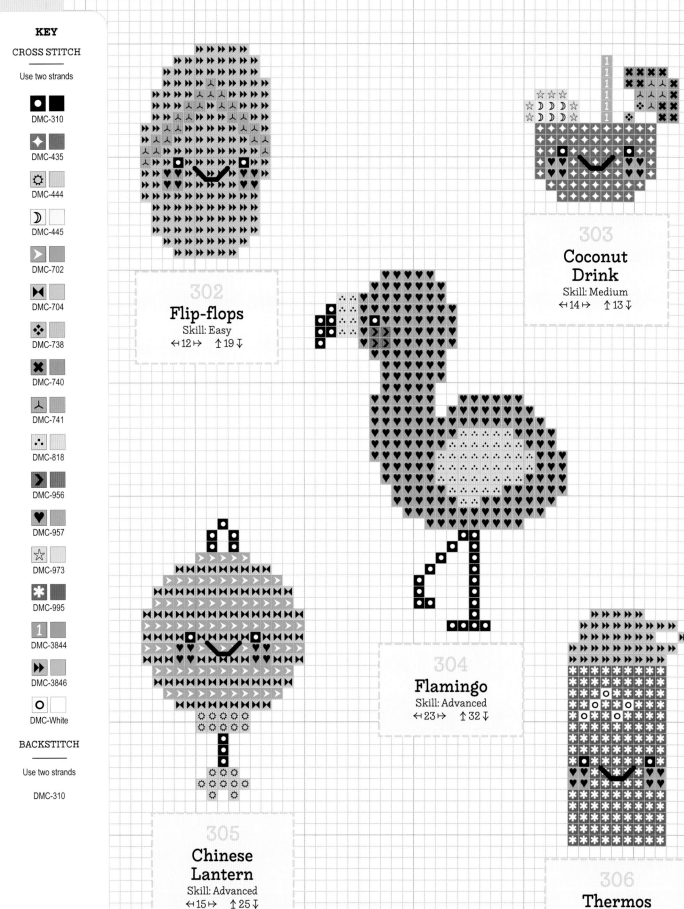

KEY

CROSS STITCH

Use two strands

⬤ ⬛ DMC-310

✦ ◢ DMC-435

☼ ▢ DMC-444

☽ ▢ DMC-445

▶ ▢ DMC-702

◀▶ ▢ DMC-704

❖ ▢ DMC-738

✖ ▢ DMC-740

⅄ ▢ DMC-741

∴ ▢ DMC-818

❯ ▨ DMC-956

♥ ▢ DMC-957

☆ ▢ DMC-973

✳ ▨ DMC-995

1 ▨ DMC-3844

▶▶ ▨ DMC-3846

○ ▢ DMC-White

BACKSTITCH

Use two strands

DMC-310

302
Flip-flops
Skill: Easy
←12↦   ↑19↓

303
Coconut Drink
Skill: Medium
←14↦   ↑13↓

304
Flamingo
Skill: Advanced
←23↦   ↑32↓

305
Chinese Lantern
Skill: Advanced
←15↦   ↑25↓

306
Thermos
Skill: Medium
←11↦   ↑21↓

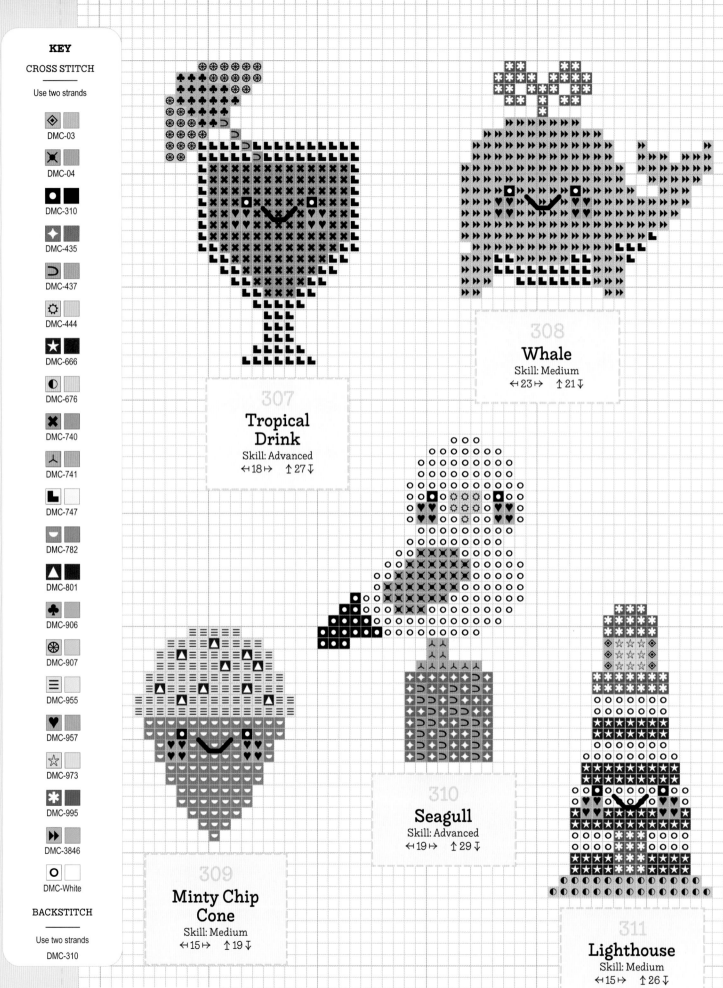

KEY

CROSS STITCH

Use two strands

◈	DMC-03
✖	DMC-04
●	DMC-310
✦	DMC-435
⊃	DMC-437
☼	DMC-444
★	DMC-666
◑	DMC-676
✖	DMC-740
⊥	DMC-741
∟	DMC-747
▭	DMC-782
△	DMC-801
♣	DMC-906
⊛	DMC-907
≡	DMC-955
♥	DMC-957
☆	DMC-973
✲	DMC-995
▶▶	DMC-3846
○	DMC-White

BACKSTITCH

Use two strands

DMC-310

307

Tropical Drink
Skill: Advanced
←18→ ↑27↓

308

Whale
Skill: Medium
←23→ ↑21↓

309

Minty Chip Cone
Skill: Medium
←15→ ↑19↓

310

Seagull
Skill: Advanced
←19→ ↑29↓

311

Lighthouse
Skill: Medium
←15→ ↑26↓

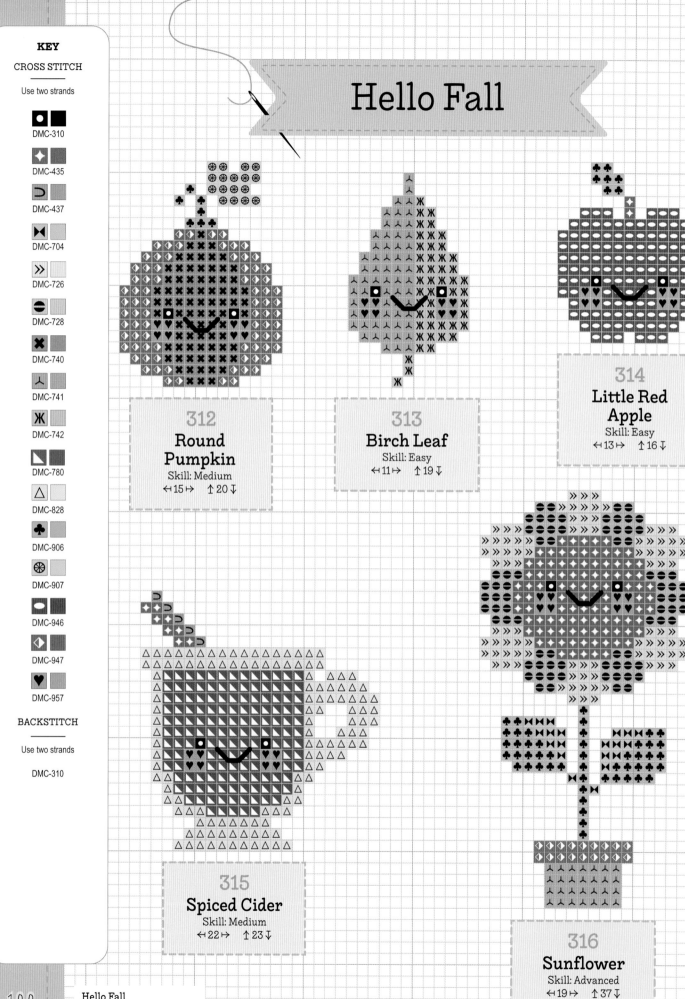

Hello Fall

KEY

CROSS STITCH

Use two strands

DMC-310
DMC-435
DMC-437
DMC-704
DMC-726
DMC-728
DMC-740
DMC-741
DMC-742
DMC-780
DMC-828
DMC-906
DMC-907
DMC-946
DMC-947
DMC-957

BACKSTITCH

Use two strands

DMC-310

312
Round Pumpkin
Skill: Medium
←15↦ ↥20↧

313
Birch Leaf
Skill: Easy
←11↦ ↥19↧

314
Little Red Apple
Skill: Easy
←13↦ ↥16↧

315
Spiced Cider
Skill: Medium
←22↦ ↥23↧

316
Sunflower
Skill: Advanced
←19↦ ↥37↧

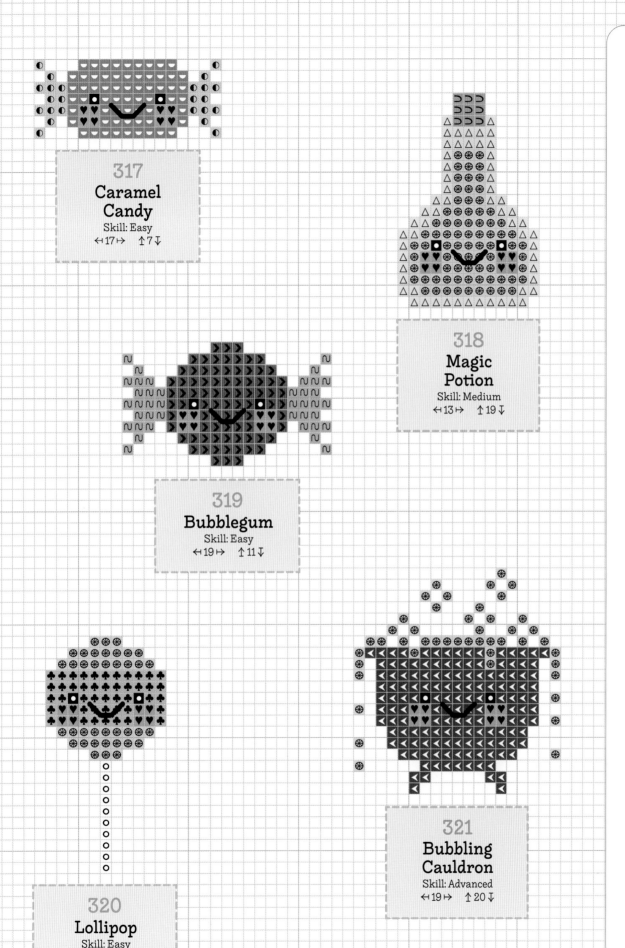

317
Caramel Candy
Skill: Easy
←17↦   ↑7↓

318
Magic Potion
Skill: Medium
←13↦   ↑19↓

319
Bubblegum
Skill: Easy
←19↦   ↑11↓

320
Lollipop
Skill: Easy
←11↦   ↑21↓

321
Bubbling Cauldron
Skill: Advanced
←19↦   ↑20↓

KEY

CROSS STITCH

Use two strands

◈	DMC-03
◐■	DMC-310
◆	DMC-435
⊃	DMC-437
◑	DMC-676
»	DMC-726
✖	DMC-740
⅄	DMC-741
✳	DMC-745
⅄	DMC-746
⊖	DMC-782
△	DMC-828
⬆	DMC-905
◈	DMC-947
♥	DMC-957

BACKSTITCH

Use two strands

DMC-310

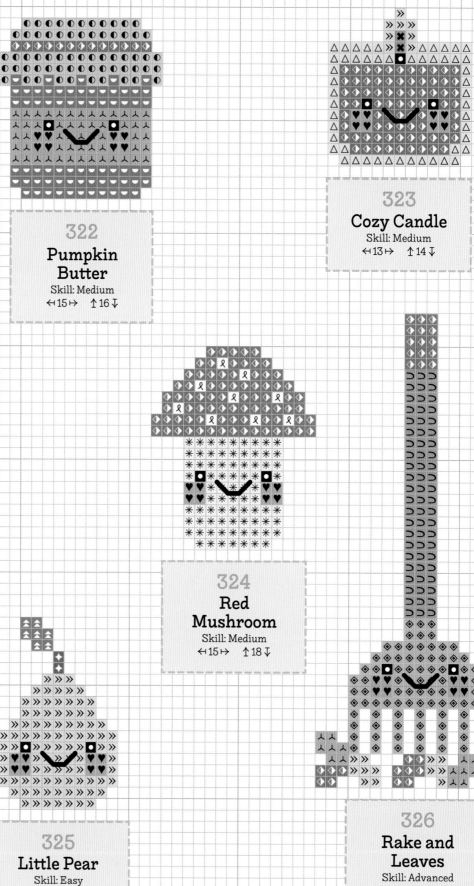

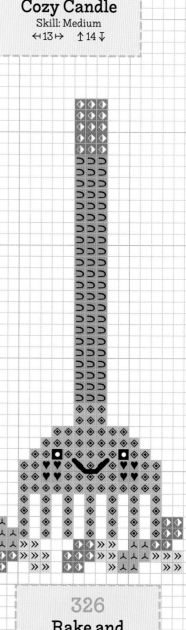

322
Pumpkin Butter
Skill: Medium
←15↦   ↑16↓

323
Cozy Candle
Skill: Medium
←13↦   ↑14↓

324
Red Mushroom
Skill: Medium
←15↦   ↑18↓

325
Little Pear
Skill: Easy
←11↦   ↑17↓

326
Rake and Leaves
Skill: Advanced
←18↦   ↑42↓

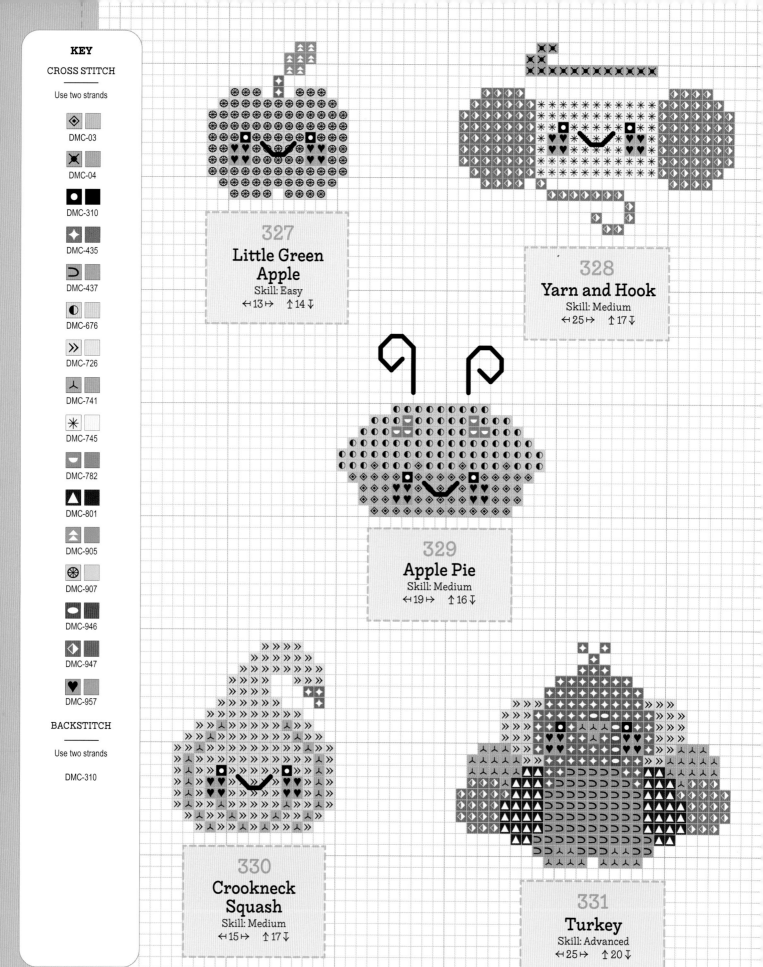

KEY

CROSS STITCH

Use two strands

DMC-03
DMC-04
DMC-310
DMC-435
DMC-437
DMC-676
DMC-726
DMC-741
DMC-745
DMC-782
DMC-801
DMC-905
DMC-907
DMC-946
DMC-947
DMC-957

BACKSTITCH

Use two strands

DMC-310

327
Little Green Apple
Skill: Easy
←13→ ↑14↓

328
Yarn and Hook
Skill: Medium
←25→ ↑17↓

329
Apple Pie
Skill: Medium
←19→ ↑16↓

330
Crookneck Squash
Skill: Medium
←15→ ↑17↓

331
Turkey
Skill: Advanced
←25→ ↑20↓

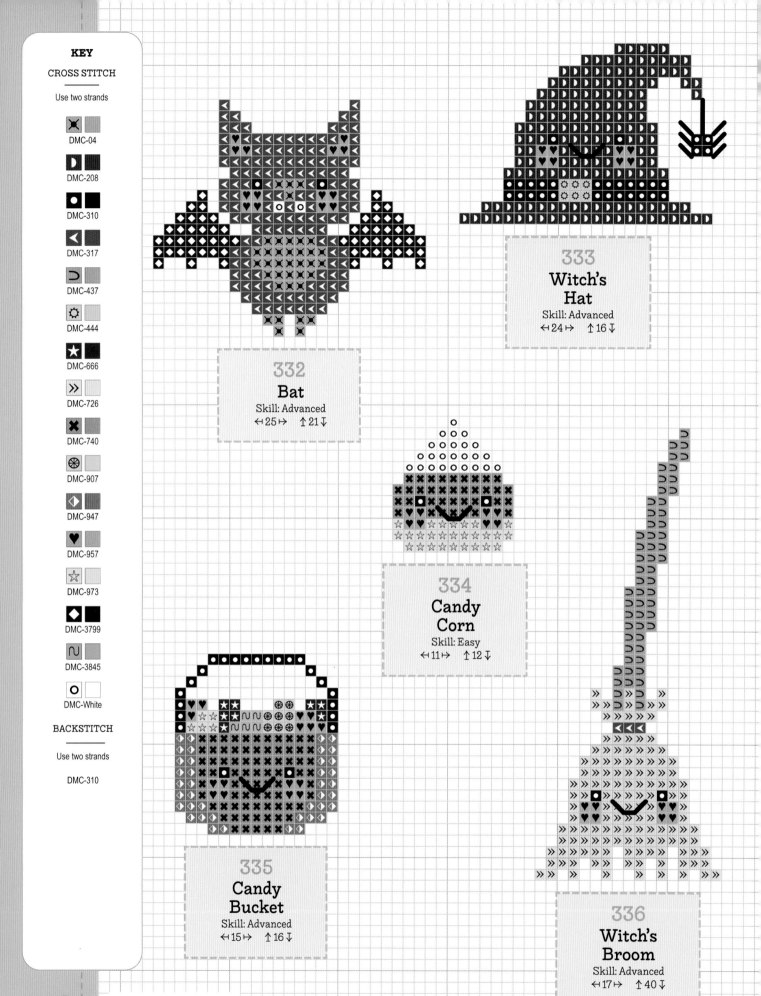

KEY

CROSS STITCH

Use two strands

DMC-04
DMC-208
DMC-310
DMC-317
DMC-437
DMC-444
DMC-666
DMC-726
DMC-740
DMC-907
DMC-947
DMC-957
DMC-973
DMC-3799
DMC-3845
DMC-White

BACKSTITCH

Use two strands

DMC-310

332
Bat
Skill: Advanced
←25↦   ↑21↓

333
Witch's Hat
Skill: Advanced
←24↦   ↑16↓

334
Candy Corn
Skill: Easy
←11↦   ↑12↓

335
Candy Bucket
Skill: Advanced
←15↦   ↑16↓

336
Witch's Broom
Skill: Advanced
←17↦   ↑40↓

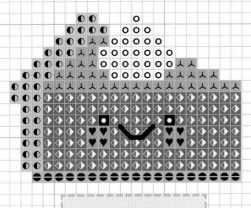

337
Pumpkin Pie Slice
Skill: Medium
←21↦ ↑15↓

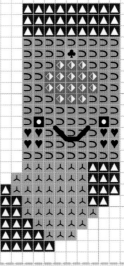

338
Cozy Socks
Skill: Medium
←12↦ ↑22↓

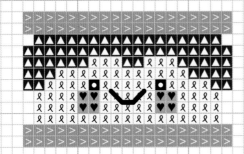

339
S'more
Skill: Medium
←19↦ ↑12↓

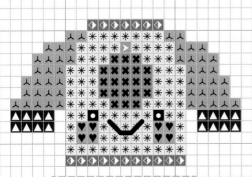

340
Autumn Sweater
Skill: Medium
←21↦ ↑13↓

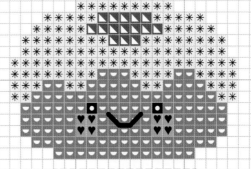

341
Maple Donut
Skill: Medium
←21↦ ↑14↓

KEY

CROSS STITCH

Use two strands

 DMC-310

 DMC-437

 DMC-676

 DMC-702

 DMC-728

 DMC-740

 DMC-741

 DMC-745

 DMC-746

 DMC-780

 DMC-782

 DMC-783

 DMC-801

 DMC-906

 DMC-947

 DMC-957

 DMC-White

BACKSTITCH

Use two strands

DMC-310

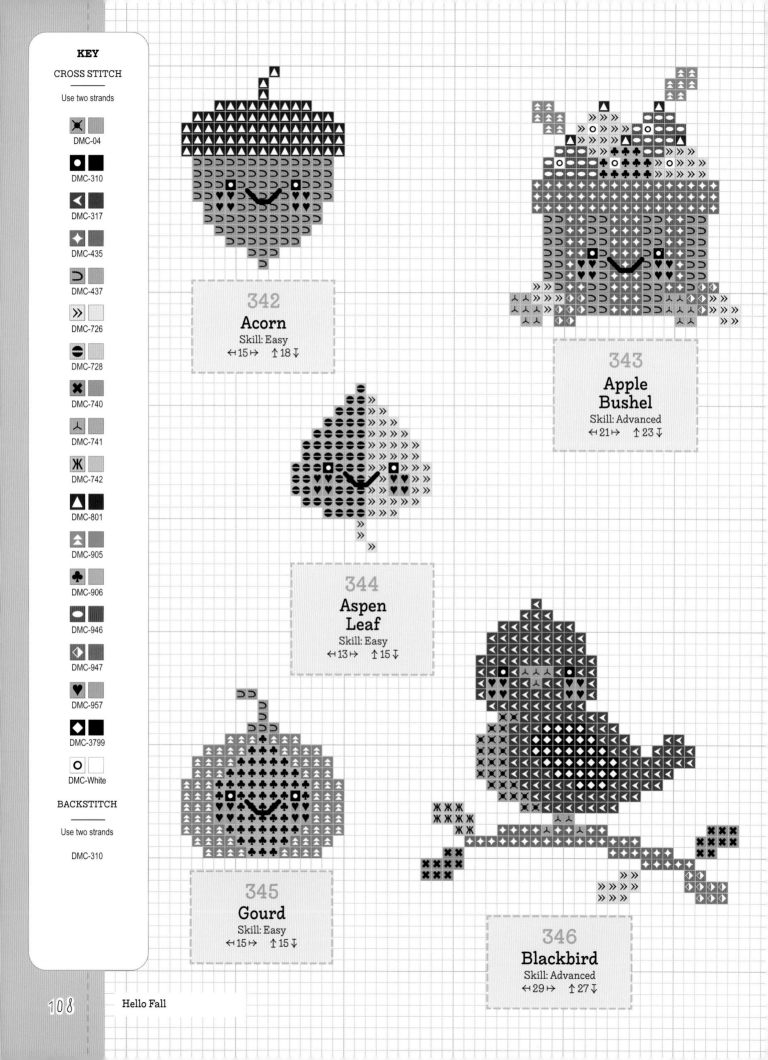

KEY

CROSS STITCH

Use two strands

DMC-04

DMC-310

DMC-317

DMC-435

DMC-437

DMC-726

DMC-728

DMC-740

DMC-741

DMC-742

DMC-801

DMC-905

DMC-906

DMC-946

DMC-947

DMC-957

DMC-3799

DMC-White

BACKSTITCH

Use two strands

DMC-310

342
Acorn
Skill: Easy
←15→ ↑18↓

343
Apple
Bushel
Skill: Advanced
←21→ ↑23↓

344
Aspen
Leaf
Skill: Easy
←13→ ↑15↓

345
Gourd
Skill: Easy
←15→ ↑15↓

346
Blackbird
Skill: Advanced
←29→ ↑27↓

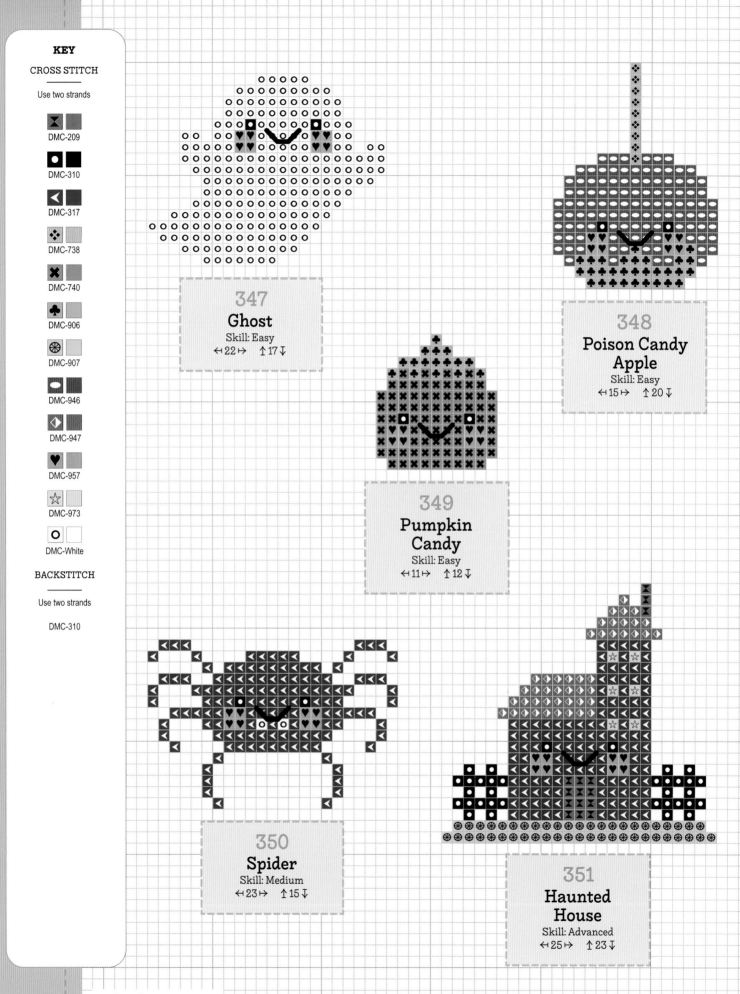

KEY

CROSS STITCH

Use two strands

DMC-209

DMC-310

DMC-317

DMC-738

DMC-740

DMC-906

DMC-907

DMC-946

DMC-947

DMC-957

DMC-973

DMC-White

BACKSTITCH

Use two strands

DMC-310

347
Ghost
Skill: Easy
←22↦ ↑17↓

348
Poison Candy
Apple
Skill: Easy
←15↦ ↑20↓

349
Pumpkin
Candy
Skill: Easy
←11↦ ↑12↓

350
Spider
Skill: Medium
←23↦ ↑15↓

351
Haunted
House
Skill: Advanced
←25↦ ↑23↓

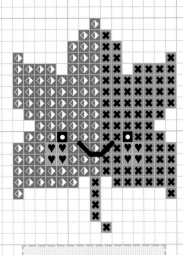

352
Maple Leaf
Skill: Easy
←15→ ↑19↓

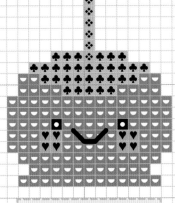

354
Caramel Apple
Skill: Easy
←15→ ↑20↓

353
Golden Mushroom
Skill: Medium
←15→ ↑14↓

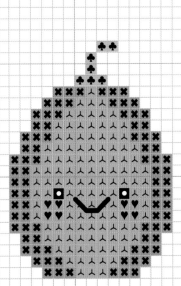

355
Tall Pumpkin
Skill: Medium
←15→ ↑21↓

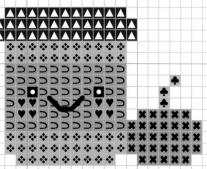

356
Pumpkin Spice Latte
Skill: Medium
←19→ ↑22↓

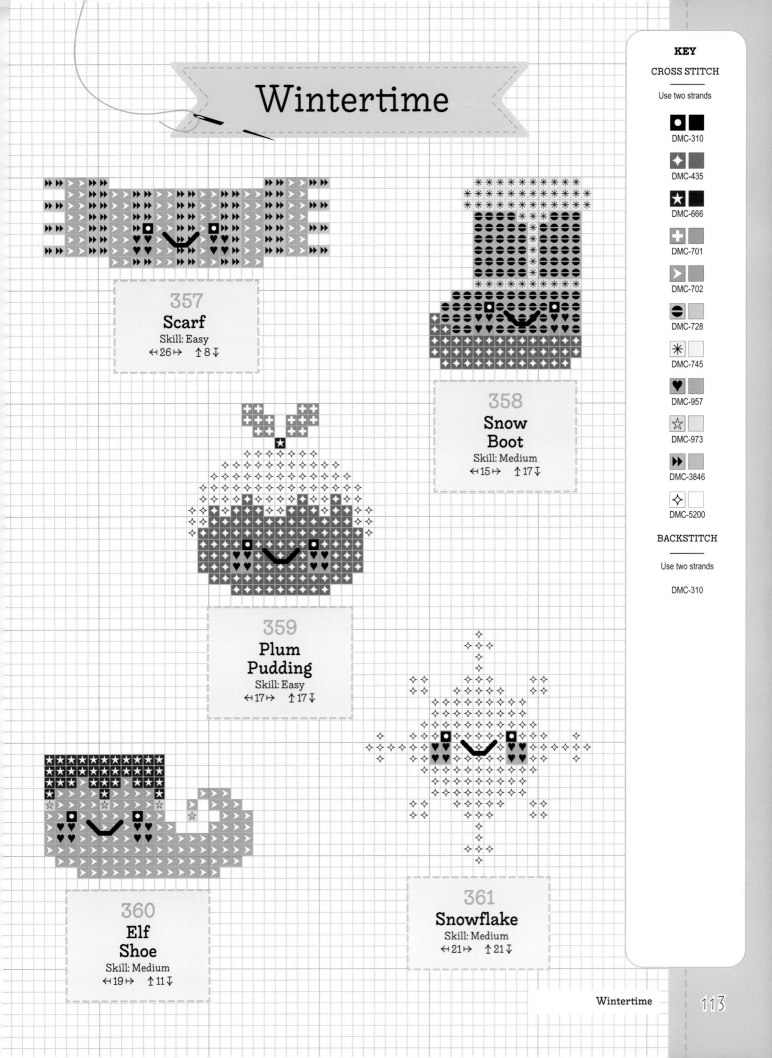

Wintertime

357
Scarf
Skill: Easy
←26→ ↑8↓

358
Snow Boot
Skill: Medium
←15→ ↑17↓

359
Plum Pudding
Skill: Easy
←17→ ↑17↓

360
Elf Shoe
Skill: Medium
←19→ ↑11↓

361
Snowflake
Skill: Medium
←21→ ↑21↓

KEY

CROSS STITCH

Use two strands

DMC-310
DMC-435
DMC-666
DMC-701
DMC-702
DMC-728
DMC-745
DMC-957
DMC-973
DMC-3846
DMC-5200

BACKSTITCH

Use two strands

DMC-310

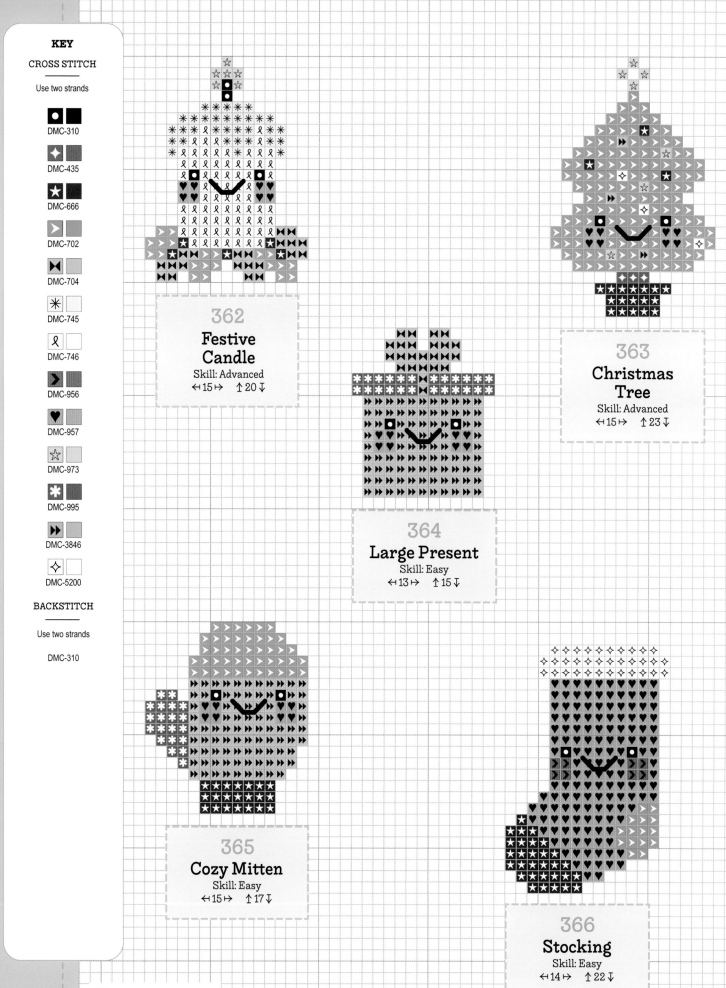

KEY

CROSS STITCH

Use two strands

DMC-310
DMC-435
DMC-666
DMC-702
DMC-704
DMC-745
DMC-746
DMC-956
DMC-957
DMC-973
DMC-995
DMC-3846
DMC-5200

BACKSTITCH

Use two strands

DMC-310

362
Festive Candle
Skill: Advanced
←15↦ ↑20↓

363
Christmas Tree
Skill: Advanced
←15↦ ↑23↓

364
Large Present
Skill: Easy
←13↦ ↑15↓

365
Cozy Mitten
Skill: Easy
←15↦ ↑17↓

366
Stocking
Skill: Easy
←14↦ ↑22↓

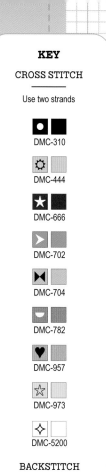

KEY

CROSS STITCH

Use two strands

DMC-310

DMC-444

DMC-666

DMC-702

DMC-704

DMC-782

DMC-957

DMC-973

DMC-5200

BACKSTITCH

Use two strands

DMC-310

367
Elf's Hat
Skill: Easy
←17→ ↑14↓

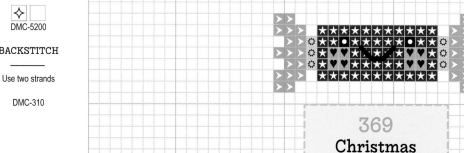

368
Santa's Sleigh
Skill: Medium
←21→ ↑13↓

369
Christmas Cracker
Skill: Easy
←19→ ↑7↓

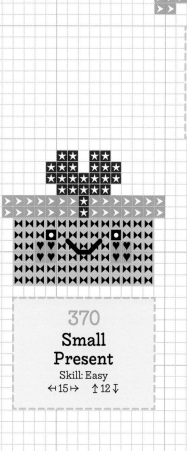

370
Small Present
Skill: Easy
←15→ ↑12↓

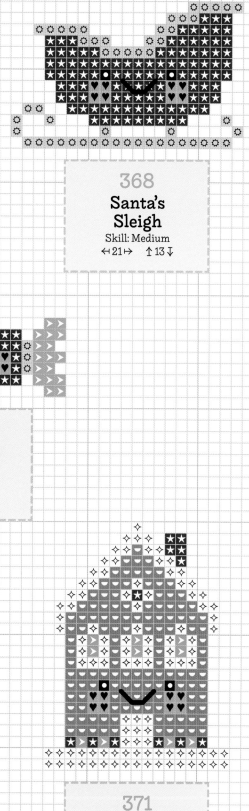

371
Gingerbread House
Skill: Advanced
←17→ ↑22↓

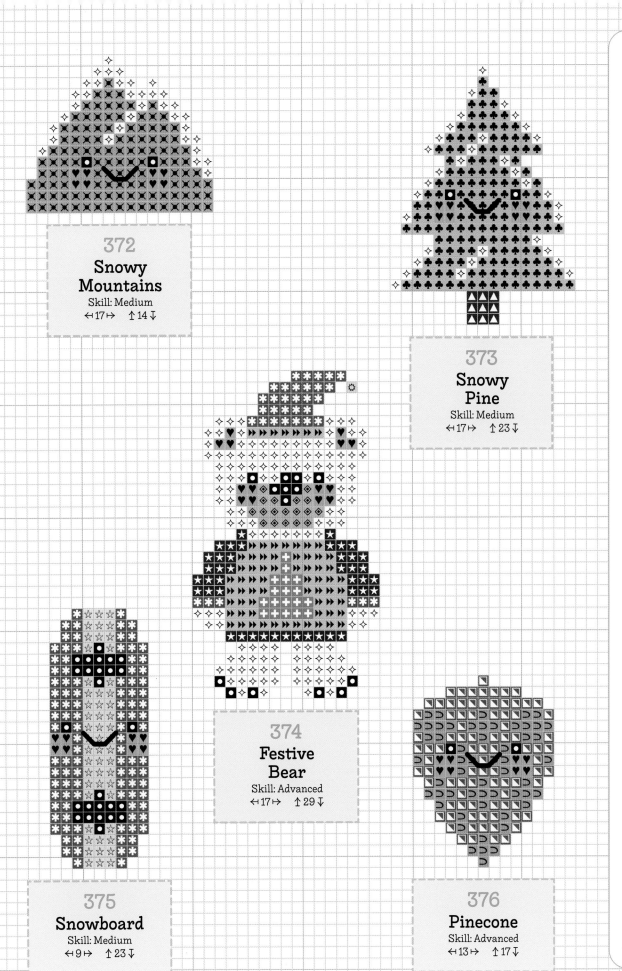

372
Snowy Mountains
Skill: Medium
←17↦ ↑14↓

373
Snowy Pine
Skill: Medium
←17↦ ↑23↓

374
Festive Bear
Skill: Advanced
←17↦ ↑29↓

375
Snowboard
Skill: Medium
←9↦ ↑23↓

376
Pinecone
Skill: Advanced
←13↦ ↑17↓

KEY

CROSS STITCH

Use two strands

 DMC-03

 DMC-04

 DMC-310

 DMC-434

 DMC-437

 DMC-444

 DMC-666

 DMC-701

 DMC-801

 DMC-906

 DMC-957

 DMC-973

 DMC-995

 DMC-3846

 DMC-5200

BACKSTITCH

Use two strands

DMC-310

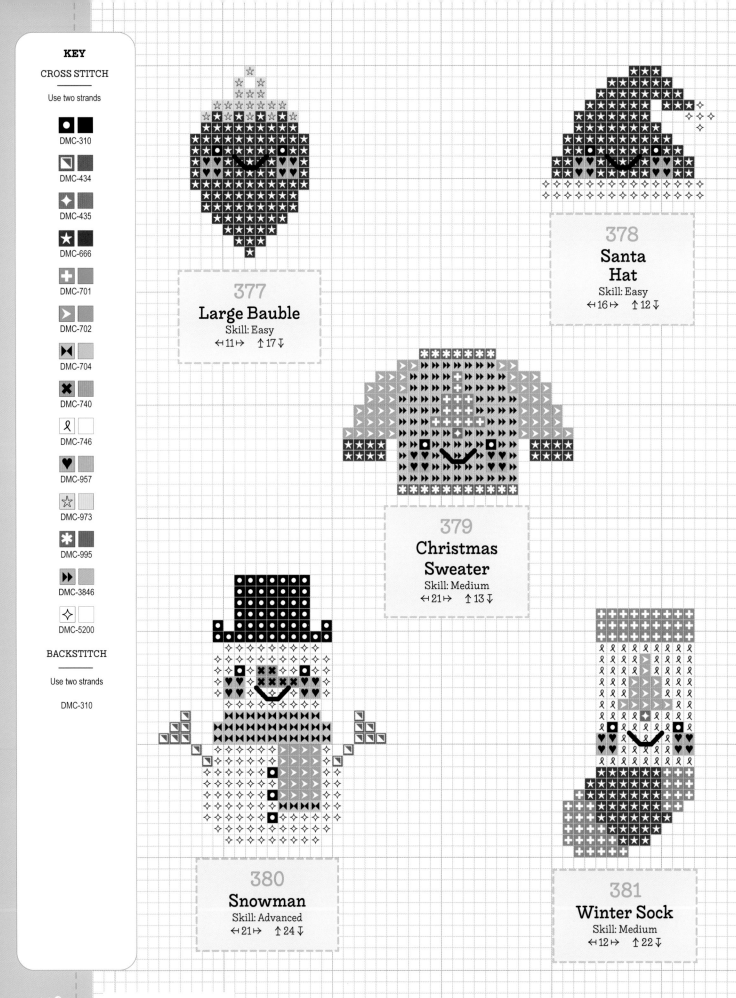

KEY

CROSS STITCH

Use two strands

DMC-310

DMC-434

DMC-435

DMC-666

DMC-701

DMC-702

DMC-704

DMC-740

DMC-746

DMC-957

DMC-973

DMC-995

DMC-3846

DMC-5200

BACKSTITCH

Use two strands

DMC-310

377
Large Bauble
Skill: Easy
←11→   ↑17↓

378
Santa Hat
Skill: Easy
←16→   ↑12↓

379
Christmas Sweater
Skill: Medium
←21→   ↑13↓

380
Snowman
Skill: Advanced
←21→   ↑24↓

381
Winter Sock
Skill: Medium
←12→   ↑22↓

KEY

CROSS STITCH

Use two strands

DMC-03

DMC-04

DMC-310

DMC-435

DMC-444

DMC-666

DMC-702

DMC-957

DMC-973

DMC-995

DMC-3846

DMC-5200

BACKSTITCH

Use two strands

DMC-310

382
Snuggly Beanie
Skill: Easy
←13↦ ↑12↓

383
Small Bauble
Skill: Easy
←11↦ ↑13↓

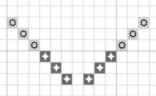

384
Festive Drum
Skill: Medium
←15↦ ↑18↓

385
Christmas Cake
Skill: Medium
←13↦ ↑17↓

386
Winter Shovel
Skill: Medium
←19↦ ↑37↓

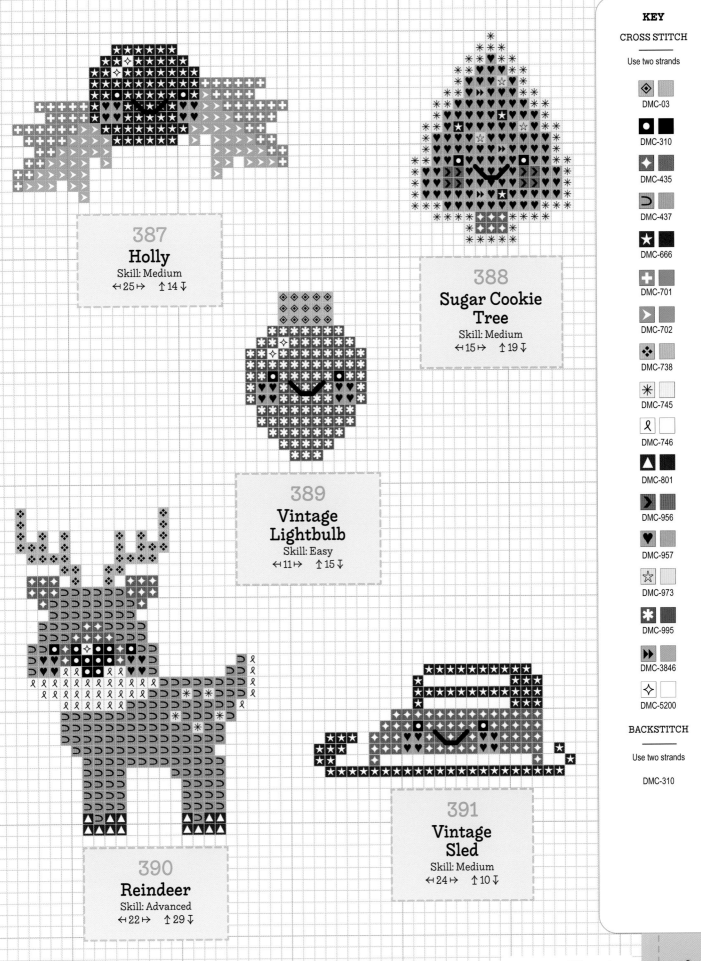

387
Holly
Skill: Medium
←25→ ↑14↓

388
Sugar Cookie Tree
Skill: Medium
←15→ ↑19↓

389
Vintage Lightbulb
Skill: Easy
←11→ ↑15↓

390
Reindeer
Skill: Advanced
←22→ ↑29↓

391
Vintage Sled
Skill: Medium
←24→ ↑10↓

KEY

CROSS STITCH

Use two strands

◈	DMC-03
●	DMC-310
✦	DMC-435
⊐	DMC-437
★	DMC-666
✚	DMC-701
▶	DMC-702
❖	DMC-738
✳	DMC-745
ℓ	DMC-746
▲	DMC-801
▶	DMC-956
♥	DMC-957
☆	DMC-973
✳	DMC-995
▶▶	DMC-3846
◇	DMC-5200

BACKSTITCH

Use two strands

DMC-310

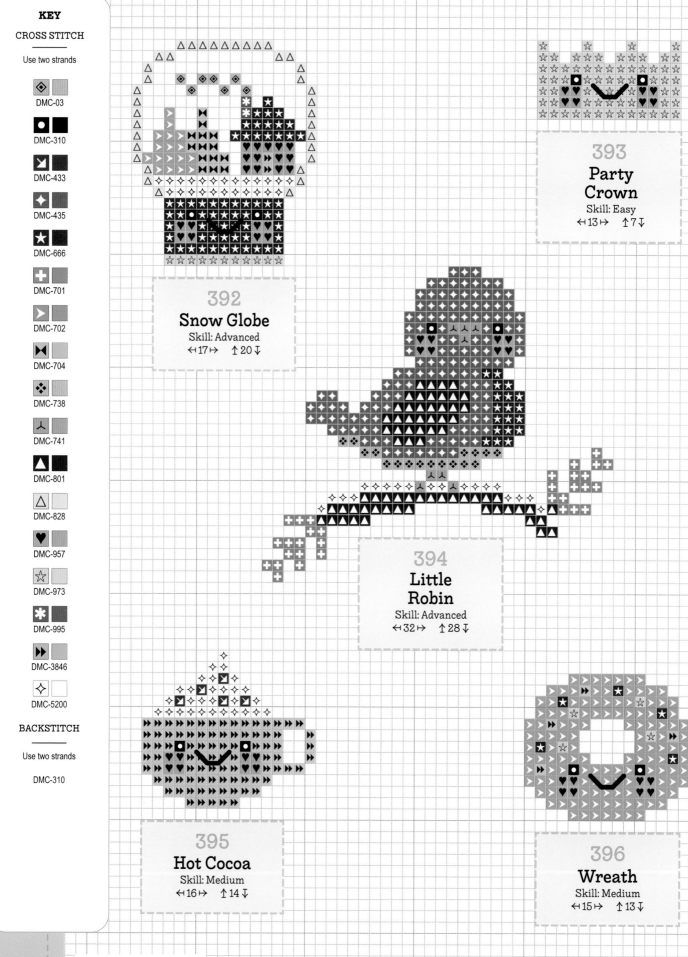

KEY

CROSS STITCH

Use two strands

◈ DMC-03

● DMC-310

◥ DMC-433

✦ DMC-435

★ DMC-666

✚ DMC-701

▶ DMC-702

◄► DMC-704

❖ DMC-738

⊥ DMC-741

▲ DMC-801

△ DMC-828

♥ DMC-957

☆ DMC-973

✳ DMC-995

▶▶ DMC-3846

◇ DMC-5200

BACKSTITCH

Use two strands

DMC-310

392
Snow Globe
Skill: Advanced
←17→ ↑20↓

393
Party Crown
Skill: Easy
←13→ ↑7↓

394
Little Robin
Skill: Advanced
←32→ ↑28↓

395
Hot Cocoa
Skill: Medium
←16→ ↑14↓

396
Wreath
Skill: Medium
←15→ ↑13↓

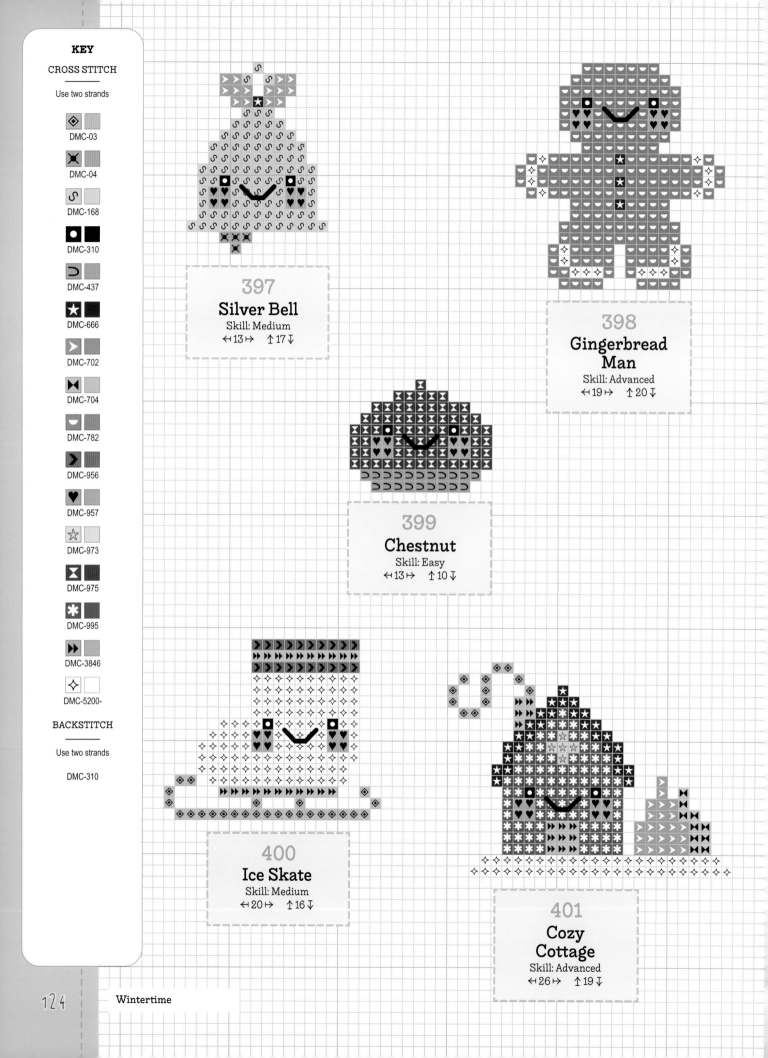

KEY

CROSS STITCH

Use two strands

◈	DMC-03
✖	DMC-04
∽	DMC-168
●	DMC-310
⊃	DMC-437
★	DMC-666
▶	DMC-702
◄►	DMC-704
�	DMC-782
▶	DMC-956
♥	DMC-957
☆	DMC-973
✕	DMC-975
✳	DMC-995
▶▶	DMC-3846
◇	DMC-5200-

BACKSTITCH

Use two strands

DMC-310

397
Silver Bell
Skill: Medium
←13→ ↑17↓

398
Gingerbread Man
Skill: Advanced
←19→ ↑20↓

399
Chestnut
Skill: Easy
←13→ ↑10↓

400
Ice Skate
Skill: Medium
←20→ ↑16↓

401
Cozy Cottage
Skill: Advanced
←26→ ↑19↓

Index

Acknowledgments

To David and Charles, our publisher, thank you.
We're proud to be a part of your fine catalog.

Our most heartfelt thanks to Quarto Publishing, and our amazing
editor, Charlene Fernandes, who guides with a gentle hand, and is always
full of encouragement. And to Martina Calvio, and the Quarto team, for
doing an epic job—the book is prettier and more charming than we could ever
imagine. And with great appreciation for Kate Kirby, who believed in us.

To the fans of Trellis & Thyme, and all our crafty endeavors—from the bottom
of our hearts, thank you. You've made our work a joy. With each little kawaii
face you stitch, there's one more smile on the earth.

And to Coolba, Fluffo, and Little Ricky—our own little kawaii cuties.
You make our home a very happy place.